SIT AND GROW RICH

SIT AND GROW RICH

Petsitting and Housesitting for Profit

PATRICIA A. DOYLE

UPSTART PUBLISHING CO., INC.
The Small Business Publishing Company
Dover, New Hampshire

Published by Upstart Publishing Company, Inc.
A Division of Dearborn Publishing Group, Inc.
12 Portland Street
Dover, New Hampshire 03820
(800) 235-8866 or (603) 749-5071

Neither the author nor the publisher of this book is engaged in rendering, by the
sale of this book, legal, accounting or other professional services. The reader is
encouraged to employ the services of a competent professional in such matters.

Library of Congress Cataloging-in-Publication Data
insert

Cover design by Acanthus Graphic Design, Newington, NH.
Cover illustration by Jennifer DeMarco © 1993. Used by kind permission of the
artist.

Printed in the United States of America
10 9 8 7 6 5 4 3 2 1

For a complete catalog of Upstart's small business publications, call (800) 235-8866.

This book is dedicated to
the loving memory of my
mother, my partner,

ALICE S. DOYLE.

Her endless love and devotion,
her absolute faith in me
that I would succeed and prosper
as only a mother's love could inspire,
will always be the cornerstone of
my lifelong endeavors.

Table of Contents

Foreword

From my first meeting with the author of this book, I knew Patricia Doyle and I would be close friends. She had the curiosity of a cat, the radiant good cheer of a skilled salesperson, and a love for animals that just would not quit. She possessed the uncanny ability to make things happen by the sheer force of her personality and by the aura of kindness that she exuded in her interactions with people. Her ideas were refreshing and her entrepreneurial spirit always inspired me. At the same time, her determination and focus set her apart from anyone I had met before. She had the unusual foresight to assimilate future needs and would use me as a sounding board as her ideas flowed ever so fluently throughout our years spent together.

Patricia moved from home in Westchester County, New York, to sunny south Florida at age 11 where she attended grade school, high school and college. The out-of-doors lifestyle served to encourage an interest in the animal kingdom and helped introduce her to a variety of opportunities to work in settings caring for domestic pets. She worked at pet shops, became a dog groomer and volunteered her time to help at animal shelters and pet care facilities. She was always close to animals and knew their needs.

Nonetheless, it came as no small surprise when Patricia developed the concept of a petsitting and housesitting service. It matched her interests and built squarely upon her experience. The surprise was that something so exciting and so enthusiastically pursued would also be profitable. In short order, I was on board the petsitting train to prosperity. With Patricia's guidance, I operated a successful branch of the petsitting and housesitting enterprise on the opposite coast in Tampa, Florida, where I was attending college.

Patricia prepared business forms, procedures and instructions that helped the new business to prosper. And it did prosper! The services offered were desperately needed and were valued by pet owners and homeowners everywhere.

From personal experience, I know that the *Sit and Grow Rich* plan works and that it includes all of the necessary ingredients to develop and operate a successful petsitting and housesitting service. This is a business that can be operated out of your home on a full-time or part-time basis. I found it to be an excellent means of financing my own college education.

The business plan and the tools to its implementation are now included in this reader-friendly guide. Each chapter outlines the exact steps needed. From business forms and sample newsletters to advertising promotions, Patricia's professional approach is succinctly set out in *Sit and Grow Rich*.

By formulating a simple plan, following detailed instructions and employing tested and proven methods, the prospective business owner can turn a love of animals into a profitable business venture. I have found this to be true and I know you will also.

—Michelle M. Dorsey
Doctor of Dental Medicine
Fort Lauderdale, Florida

"Follow your dreams
and pursue them with courage,
for it is the pursuit
of those dreams that makes
life really worth living."

—*Linda Dupuy Moore*

Introduction

Welcome to the unique and rewarding world of petsitting and housesitting! Home-to-home petsitting and housesitting is an extraordinary business opportunity built upon love and care of animals. If you are looking for a home-based business with extremely low start-up costs and a healthy profit potential, this is it! The sky is the limit with this unique service business. By purchasing *Sit and Grow Rich*, you have invested wisely in your future. The unlimited income earning potential and the idea of starting your own business with virtually no specialized training has immediate appeal to people of all ages. Caring for animals is one of the most emotionally fulfilling careers in today's workplace. Your business can be anything from a part-time endeavor bringing you a few thousand dollars per year or it can be a full-time business enterprise generating more than you could imagine!

Owning and operating your own business is an exhilarating yet demanding experience. If you sincerely want freedom and independence, then "being your own boss" is the way to go. Turn your dreams into reality. Owning and operating your own business means having the best of both worlds. It is for anyone who has dreamed of economic security, more free time and a healthier, more productive lifestyle. You become the creator of each and every day of your working life, shaping it instead of reacitng to it. Flexibility and variety are what make your success all the more rewarding. You set your own hours, plan your daily direction. One hundred percent of how you strategically plan and control your work day navigates your individual course to freedom and wealth, both monetarily and personally. For those who want to take charge of their day-to-day lives and futures, this is the only way to go. My manual and forms increase your likelihood of attaining prosperity and contentment. I provide the step-by-step instructions to guide you.

As far back as I can remember, I had always dreamed of working with animals. I was profoundly touched by the unconditional love they provide and their total dependence on humans to maintain their health and, in fact, their very existence. I knew one day I would incorporate the care of animals into my life. Fortunately, my petsitting idea proved to be a timely arrival. Throughout my five years of petsitting, I have witnessed and experienced some of the most profound and meaningful events of my life. Caring for animals has completely enriched my life. It has re-introduced me to the true meaning of compassion, kindness and selflessness. Working with animals is a definite learning experience. It is amusing and entertaining but must be regarded as a serious occupation.

I know first hand that petsitting is profitable and enjoyable. I started my own successful petsitting and housewatching service in 1985. It grew to be the largest petsitting operation in the south Florida area! I also created a branch office on the northwest coast of Florida and expanded my horizons by servicing northern Florida as well as southern Florida.

At the time I began my petsitting service, I was working as a real estate agent in Boca Raton, Florida. Beautiful homes, wonderful clientele, and an opportunity to make alot of money. However, something was missing. Although it was a lucrative profession, it lacked the personal satisfaction that I had known in the past while working with animals. The idea for petsitting grew out of doing favors for my friends. I took care of their pets while they were away on weekend trips and vacations. Some friends ACTUALLY had me going to their homes five and six times a day!. "I should really charge them for this!" I said to myself. That's when the wheels started turning and my success story began.

I placed a small classified ad in my neighborhood newspaper. I never dreamed it was to be the beginning of a five-year flourishing enterprise! Phone calls were pouring in from everywhere inquiring about my new service sensation! Luckily, my mother came to my rescue. She assisted me by answering the telephone calls, setting up appointments and mailing out customer information packages. I met with the customers and their pets and signed them up! I could not believe the extraordinary response. My business grew to over 350 customers within a five year period. Of course I made mistakes, but I learned from every one of them. I relentlessly forged ahead until I mastered the petsitting service concept.

Petsitting is so much more than walking a dog or feeding a cat. The gratification is incomparable. You must be committed and dedicated to your profession. You achieve personal satisfaction from the happiness you spread to those who truly need your help. There are multitudes of concerned pet owners seeking a kennel alternative. Many of my customers refuse to take vacations or trips because they can't bear to put their pets in a kennel. Imposing on friends and family members was totally out of the question. They sacrificed THEIR happiness for the sake of their pets. Only a competent petsitter can fill this void for pet owners.

Pet owners take vacations at least once a year and make countless business trips. Who, then, will feed and walk the dog, change the litter box and give Polly a cracker? YOU WILL! In the past, the only alternatives available to traveling pet owners were kennels and boarding facilities. NO MORE! Home-to-home petsitting services are the most innovative and prosperous fields of pet care today! They are a professional convenience. They offer an unparalleled commodity to pet owners everywhere: peace of mind.

Petsitting's popularity stems from the many attractive features it offers to pet owners. Domestic pets are cared for in their own familiar surroundings, "HOME SWEET HOME." Pets are cared for in their own homes and their schedules are maintained, thus reducing stress and preserving their contentment. Petsitters also bring much needed security to the home by providing that lived-in look that deters burglars. They can visit 15 to 20 homes during an average day, charging upwards of $15.00 per visit. A petsitter's income can average over $300.00 per day! Whether you choose to petsit on a part-time or full-time basis, the benefits are well worth the effort. Dedication, integrity, professionalism and patience are the inherent values you must possess to succeed.

Pet ownership has been in existence since the beginning of time. It is a proven fact that pet owners consider their pets as family members. About 80 percent of pet owners talk to their pets. The majority of pet owners let their pets sleep with them. Pets provide beneficial, medical and physiological effects such as lowering blood pressure and alleviating stress. Pets convey a sense of security and continuity. Therapeutically speaking, pets actually motivate people to play, exercise and, astonishingly enough, help raise self-esteem and self-worth. Pets are loyal, devoted freinds. They are faithful companions for life. Plain and simple, PEOPLE LOVE PETS! In return for their pet's devotion, pet owners demand the very best care for their pets. This includes the specialized attention that must be provided when they are away from home. THE NEED FOR PERSONALIZED PET SERVICES IS ON THE RISE!

Petsitters are welcome newcomers to the service business industry, which has become the fastest growing industry in the United States today. Every economic indicator points to the service industry boom! Coupled with the overwhelming demand for petsitters and the fact that pet owners spend over $8 billion dollars a year for their well being, petsitters are virtually spearheading a pivotal trend in the service industry today. They will play an integral part in America's future economic growth. The *Occupational Outlook Handbook,* assembled by the Bureau of Labor Statistics, distributes economic surveys pertaining to the labor market. This is an informative tool for the small business owner. For further information on this subject, write to: *Occupational Outlook Handbook,* Superintendent of Documents, Government Printing Office, Washington, DC 20402.

In addition to the petsitting service, my housesitting or housewatching service has proved to be in very high demand across the country. You may offer this service as part of or totally separate from the pet service. Petless homeowners who travel frequently or who have summer or winter homes, condominiums, apartments or townhomes, and leave them unoccupied for long periods of time, require someone to look after the property, both inside and out. Daily, weekly or monthly checkups of the premises are necessary. It is a miniature residential property management company, fundamentally identical to petsitting minus the pets!

In closing, the happiness petsitting has brought me supersedes any other business venture I could have chosen to start. You too, will share in the realization of good fortune and financial independence. As your business grows, you may have the option to franchise your sitting service! Success or failure depends on the day-to-day management of occupational difficulties. Your ability to surpass these obstacles will enable the business to progress in the right direction. I believe each of us has a unique gift to give the world. Whatever you choose to do, DO IT WELL and DO IT NOW! Draw upon the knowledge of experts in the pet care field. They provide sound advice and support. I sincerely hope this manual will serve as a source of help and encouragement by helping you to analyze and realize your capabilities, and to constructively plan your future career. I furnish you with all the tools you need. Take them in hand and build a skyscraper of a business!! Good luck!

Chapter 1

Profitability in Petsitting

If there is a market for your business idea, the feasibility and practicalilty of your concept will go hand-in-hand with success. The petsittting service concept met all the requirements necessary for me to proceed with confidence. My very first step before plunging head first into the petsitting industry was preceded by a diligent market research study that revealed the confirmation of profitability that I needed. Statistically speaking, the petsitting concept was surely a winner.

My research revealed the following:

1. Americans own more than 1.2 trillion pets.

2. Sixty percent of all American households have some kind of pet.

3. Americans spend over eight billion dollars yearly on their pets.

4. Dollars spent on pet services are anticipated to increase by 50 percent.

5. In the 1990s, pet-related spending will increase by 14 billion dollars!

6. Service businesses are the fastest growing industries in the United States today.

7. I personally telephoned over 200 veterinarians and inquired into the needs of their customers. Their primary concern: the lack of proper care for pets while pet owners were away from home!

The market was well defined, indicating potential customers. The need was definitely there. But, could I really make a living doing this? Could I realistically support myself? I gathered information from various kennels and boarding facilities and compiled a list of prices from them. The going rate averaged $8.00 for each pet for each day they were being boarded. Knowing that the petsitting concept was so much more personalized and that there were added services for the home, I knew that I could easily charge between $12.00 to $15.00 per visit per household with unlimited pets to care for.

Income

How many households could I safely visit in one day? If I began my day at 7:00 A.M. and worked till 7:00 P.M., I could realistically visit 15 homes charging an average of $13.50 per visit. I would make around $200.00 in one day. On the down side, even if I only visited seven households per day, my income would still be able to handle the monthly expenses I would incur. It was totally up to me how much I wanted to make. See the projected income and expenses summary on the following page.

Expenses

Fixed monthly expenses will run approximately $280.00. These expenses include gasoline, car insurance, liability insurance, dishonesty bond, advertising, office supplies, telephone, licenses and permits. If you hire a part-time worker to help you out, your monthly expenses would rise about $200.00 per month, but your income ratio would rise 15 percent per month paying a part-time helper $5.00 per hour, 10 hours per week.

Start-Up Costs

Petsitting is solely a service-oriented business and the start-up costs are discretionary. However, I wanted to proceed professionally. I wanted to set myself up according to the rules and regulations of city and state government agencies. I also wanted to cover all aspects of protection for my company and myself. However, I was very frugal. I did not need to go all out and spend a lot of money on insignificant frills. I did plenty of price shopping and found the most economical ways to go. As the business grew, so would my quality of spending. I knew I had to keep costs down at first and I never wavered. My initial start-up costs included: liability insurance, business car insurance, initial office supplies including office furniture, introductory advertising costs, joining various organizations including the Better Business Bureau and the Chamber of Commerce, transferring my residential telephone line to a business line, initial Yellow Pages™ advertising costs, and maintenance supplies. Out of pocket start-up costs could be anywhere from $1,000 to $5,000. See the list I compiled in Chapter 12, The Home Office, for more ideas on what you need to get started.

The Business Plan

Income projections and an accurate, realistic overview of your anticipated growth are necessary for you to forecast realistic goals. You should come up with a detailed prognostication designed specifically to guide your business toward a proposed growth pattern. A business plan serves two functions. It can be used to develop ideas about how the business should be conducted. It is also a retrospective medium from which you can assess the business's actual performance over time. Some of the components of a good business plan are: Your objectives and milestones for the business, the marketing plan, analysis and strategy, your operational plan, timetables and schedules. Where do you want to be this time next year? How much money do you want to be making in six months? How many employees do you want to hire and when? Put your business plan together and plan your future.

Sample Projected Income Statement

For Your First Year of Petsitting

SALES OR REVENUES	$35,000
NET SALES	35,000
COST OF SALES	0
GROSS PROFIT	35,000
OPERATING EXPENSES	
Salary (you pay yourself)	25,000
Wages (your helpers)	2,400
Car insurance	600
Business insurance (liability)	500
Dishonesty bond	100
Office supplies	180
Telephone	300
Advertising	300
Gasoline	1,200
Licenses and permits	100
Other expenses (repairs, misc.)	1,000
TOTAL OPERATING EXPENSES	31,980
TOTAL OPERATING INCOME	35,100
NET PROFIT	3,120

The above projections are based on the following:

Income is derived by projecting ten petsittings per day, five days per week, at $13.50 per sit. You are paying yourself a salary of $25,000 per year. You are employing a helper, ten hours per week at $5.00 per hour.

Chapter 2

Getting Started

One of the very first steps you must take before launching your new venture is to create a name for the business. Originality and creativity are the keys to choosing the ideal name to attract customers. Before I named my company, I composed a list with over 20 selections I believed were perfect for my extraordinary idea. Family and friends also contributed ideas. Gather everyone together and play the name game!

The best name for your new business is one that **describes** your services. **Beware of unusual or unrelated names!** They will confuse potential customers and your business may go unnoticed as a petsitting service.

Develop a name that works well in a logo. Animal illustrations are abundant and can serve as guidelines. Combine them collectively with the names you choose. The name of my business was simply "Pet Sitting Services, Inc." The public definitely knew what my business was all about!

If you intend to operate your business as a sole proprietorship select any name other than your own—for example, "Petcare Services"—fictitious name registration is mandatory.

Some Sample Business Names:

Petsitters, TLC	Pet Sitting Services
Critter Sitters	Petcare Services
Pet Vacations	Sit a Pet
Pet Watchers	Feed a Pet
Pet Nanny	Pet Tenders

The preceding list of business names are merely suggestions. It is your responsibility to determine whether or not these names are available in accordance with the instructions outlined in this book.

Fictitious Name Registration

Fictitious name registration is a relatively uncomplicated procedure that is a prerequisite to operating your business. A "fictitious name " is any name that is not a given legal name under which a person transacts business. A person may not engage in business under a fictitious name unless they fulfill specific requirements. In most states, the law requires that those engaged in business using a fictitious name must publish and file a notice for general notification and recognition. You must register the name with the county and/or the state. Regulations vary nationwide. Contact the proper agencies. Refer to the Government section of your local telephone book under the following headings: city and county Building and Zoning Departments and Business Licenses and Inspection.

Florida law required publicizing the name I selected for my business in a local newspaper. The purpose for advertising the name in this manner is to be certain no other business is using the same name. If so, and they object in writing to the newspaper, then you must choose another name.

I had to publish the ad once a week for four consecutive weeks under the heading of "New Businesses." Thirty days after the publication's approval, I received a notarized Proof of Publication. The newspaper also provided an affidavit noting that the fictitious name requirements had been satisfied. The name I selected was free to use.

My next step was to record the business name with the clerk of the county court. It may be possible for you to ascertain name availability by telephoning or visiting the deeds and records division of your county courthouse. According to laws recently passed in my state, I must now file my business name with the state Division of Corporations.

The cost to advertise a fictitious name varies from newspaper to newspaper. Do some price shopping. It will cost between $30 and $50 for the four weeks of advertising. The county filing fee will be about $10 and the state filing fee, if applicable, is about $50.

If you plan to incorporate under a business name, determine name availability by calling your state Division of Corporations. You cannot patent an idea or method of doing business; however, the name you choose may be portrayed in a trademark or servicemark. A servicemark is a trademark for services.

The federal government affords legal protection for these representations. Regulated by the Commissioner of Patents and Trademarks, U.S. Department of Commerce, registering a trademark protects a name or symbol. This protection takes the form of an exclusive property right.

Trademarks remain registered for 20 years with renewal rights. You could find yourself being sued for infringement if you pick a name previously registered. To initiate a name search, call or write a letter of inquiry to: Commissioner of Patents and Trademarks, Patent and Trademark Office, Washington, D.C. 20231, (703) 557-3341. Enclose a self-addressed, stamped return envelope for an expedited response.

Specific public libraries and patent/trademark depository libraries provide access to a multitude of databases for you to execute computer information searches. Trademark searches may be performed at an hourly rate. If you choose to designate a patent attorney or patent agent to perform the search for you, the cost can range from $400 to $500. Telephone your local library for information.

Instantaneous recognition of your business is attainable if you acquire a logo or a service mark. Your logo should commuinicate to the public what your business is all about. It is your graphic identity. It can be a powerful marketing tool if it is designed with a message to attract potential petsitting customers. It should convey a clear understanding of the services you will offer and where you want your business to go. It should also define your business goals. Perhaps you may want to franchise in the future. If so, choose a logo with that in mind. What kind of logos are your competitors using? How could you do better?

Choose a logo that will distinguish and associate your business with your profession—namely, a symbol affiliated with animals and animal care. You can portray pets in countless ways. Convert them into your own personalized logo. Remember, your logo will convey a message to your prospective customers. They will probably see your logo before they see you.

If, and only if, you have artistic abilities and have a good idea of what you want your logo to be, save yourself some money and design it yourself. But commercial printers have volumes of pre-made logos, depicting a wide variety of businesses, from which to choose. College art students offer their talents at a discounted rate as opposed to an expensive graphic designer. Call your local college and inquire. When you have chosen your logo, all printed materials you distribute must exhibit the identical logo you have chosen. Customers will identify you with your logo. Type style and color should always be the same. Consistency is the key.

Sample Logo:

Chapter 3

Obtaining Proper Licenses

Operating your business within a city or a township, whether it be an urban, suburban or rural locale, necessitates getting an occupational license. The occupational license is a permit allowing you to run your business from that specific location. Your local government body grants you permission to conduct business by issuing you this license. You are subject to local regulations and zoning restrictions. You may also need a county occupational license. For information, call your city hall and county occupational licensing department. They will instruct you accordingly.

The information required when filing for your occupational license is considerable. You need to supply the business name, type of business, business location, and starting date. In addition, they need your legal name, address, telephone number, drivers license number and Social Security card. Also required is the organizational structure of your business, number of employees and related details for their records. If you are conducting business as a sole proprietorship under a fictitious name, you must bring documented proof of fictitious name registration.

If you are conducting business as a corporation, present the articles of incorporation and the corporate charter listing the officers of the corporation. They also want to know the number of employees you will or have hired. If you hire three or more employees, you will need to produce your worker's compensation insurance policy. Presumably, this will not apply to you. The yearly fee for an occupational license is between $10 and $50.

When you disclose to your customers that you have an occupational license with the city, county or state, they will see you as an established business. This boosts their confidence and trust in you.

Chapter 4

Structuring Your Business

The type of legal structure you select to govern your business operation is crucial for attaining success. You have three legal entities from which to choose: **sole proprietorship**, **partnership**, and **corporation**. First and foremost, you must consider your individual circumstances before making your decision.

Personal situations differ immensely. It is critical to examine the legal form of business that will protect you and your family if for some reason the business fails. Below, I've summarized the definition of each entity and provided some benefits and drawbacks of each.

Sole Proprietorship

A sole proprietorship is a business enterprise owned exclusively by just one person. That person controls the everyday operation of the business.

Benefits: The start-up costs are very low. You are the owner, supervisor, manager and overseer. All profits go directly to the sole proprietor. There are few organizational costs.

Drawbacks: You are personally liable for all debts and legal judgments filed against the business. If your business fails, your personal assets are at risk and can be confiscated in lieu of payment. You will perform a variety of functions from advertising to accounting. Business loans are difficult if not impossible to obtain.

Partnership

A partnership is defined as a business entity with two or more owners managing the business and dividing the profits.

Benefits: To get started is an uncomplicated process. There are low start-up costs. Tax advantages are more widespread. Partners only pay personal income tax.

Drawbacks: Partners divide the profits between themselves. The partners are personally liable for all debts and judgments filed against the business. Problems can arise between partners because the authority to make decisions is divided between them. Compatible business partners are difficult to find.

A limited partnership is a partnership consisting of one general partner and several other partners who invest money in the business but have no say in the day-to-day operations. This practice is popular for real estate syndications.

Corporation

Universally, a corporation is regarded as a separate entity created apart from those who run the business. The cost for incorporating a small business varies from approximately $100 to over $1,000. You can incorporate yourself, or pay an attorney to do it. Call your state division of corporations for instructions on self-incorporating and the fees involved. A corporation has stockholders. This means that each person who owns stock in your corporation is a co-owner with you in the business.

Your main objective for incorporating the business is to protect yourself against personal liability. If the business fails or becomes the subject of a lawsuit, only the business is at risk. Your car, your future earnings, your savings, your home or any personal assets remain unaffected. The company itself is responsible for all of its debts and actions. All debts and problems remain legally separate from you. To determine if the name you have chosen for your business is free to use, call the of state division of corporations. They will answer all questions concerning corporate status.

Benefits: Ownership is transferrable and the corporation's existence is continuous. Loans to the business may be more easily attainable. Investors and owners have limited liability.

Drawbacks: Corporations are closely regulated. The recordkeeping process is substantially increased. Initial start-up costs are relatively more expensive. Corporations experience double taxation. This means that the income generated by the corporation is taxed and the income you personally derive from the corporation is taxed also.

All businesses must apply for an Employer Identification Number. This number will identify your business by a tax number issued by the Internal Revenue Service. To receive the proper form, call the Internal Revenue Service.

It is my strong suggestion that you seek professional guidance. For more details on these business structures, contact an attorney or a certified public accountant. If you do not have an attorney, consult your telephone book under the listings, "Attorney or Lawyer Referral Services," or ask other business people for referrals.

Chapter 5

Insurance and Bonding

Dishonesty Bonds

Considering the restrictive, confidential responsibilities of your business, you must bond yourself and your workers. Dishonesty bonds protect you from accusations of stealing. In actuality, when your customers know your business has theft coverage, they feel more at ease when granting you permission to enter their homes. Dishonesty bonds also help solidify your business operation. If something were missing from a customer's home and assumed stolen, they are repaid for any losses they may sustain.

There are three parties involved with a bond:

1. **The Principal:** The person who has the original obligation (you)

2. **The Obligee:** The person to whom the obligation is owed (your customer)

3. **The Surety:** The party that guarantees the obligation (the bonding company)

A bond encompasses those events within the control of the person bonded. Insurance covers losses caused by random events outside the direct control of the insured. Do not confuse bonding with insurance coverage!! Please note: The bonding company has the right to collect its losses from the person bonded . . . you.

We trust that those we hire will perform their duties in an honest and competent manner. This is not always the case. Therefore, we must take further precautions to protect our interests as well as our customers. *Never presume anything.*

Dishonesty bonds not only cover dishonesty, but also an employee's inability to perform the work he or she has agreed to. Dishonesty bonds are surprisingly inexpensive. I paid $100 for $10,000 in bond coverage for one year. Shop around for prices.

Contact your insurance company for details on bonding. There is a wide assortment of bonds with various levels and limits of coverage. Stipulate that you are a petsitting and home care service. Define the duties you perform. A petsitting service requires essentially equivalent coverage as a dry cleaning company. Some bonding companies may characterize a petsitting service under an independent classification of its own. Whether you purchase a blanket bond or an individual bond, it must encompass all workers. Register in writing to the bonding company all names and addresses of those you wish to cover. Use Form #9 (found in the Appendix). Drop and add names accordingly.

Liability Insurance

When performing your daily duties, accidents will happen. Businesses are subject to negligence claims of countless varieties. Negligence is the failure to use proper precautions to prevent injury or harm. Whether it be property damage or bodily harm, you are the responsible party. There are those individuals who fail to act reasonably or exercise due care. In the eyes of the law, these people are subject to large liability claims.

In our case, property damage is the issue at hand. Liability insurance provides protection for you and your employees. It is compulsory in most businesses today, both large and small.

Liability insurance pays the money the insured legally owes the customer for damages incurred. It also pays the cost of defending the insured party (you). I have never had a problem with a liability or theft claim because I was extraordinarily cautious.

For my added protection, I drafted two "release of liability" forms for my customers to sign (Forms are #6 and #7). The release forms contend that your clients will not hold you liable for anything not due to your negligence. The pets we care for are in the home unsupervised for extended periods; therefore we should not be liable for any problems that occur during these specific intervals. Your commitment is to insure that all pets remain assiduously cared for as specified by the owners.

Liability insurance can be expensive. It can range from $500 to $5,000 yearly depending on the amounts and types of coverage necessary. My liability coverage cost me $500 per year and insured me up to $100,000. I suggest you obtain no less than $100,000 in liability coverage. It is not manadatory that you purchase liability insurance if you intend to work alone, but once you start hiring helpers, it is wise to protect yourself and your business from any unforeseen occurrences.

When I first started my business, I did all the petsitting myself. I was extremely careful. Be very cautious and observant in the homes you enter. If you can afford liability insurance, by all means, buy it.

Another avenue to investigate in lieu of liability insurance is to examine your own homeowners or apartment dwellers insurance policy. Some policies contain a clause providing liability coverage on any business run out of your own home. Definitely have adequate coverage on the contents of your home, including your home office equipment. Business interruption insurance is another policy that you may consider, because it provides the money you would need for fixed business expenses such as payroll, loan payments on business equipment, or whatever funds it may take to get your business back in operation should a fire or a catastrophe destroy your place of business and your ability to function as such. Keep an accurate list of all office equipment and receipts in order to file an accurate insurance claim in case of such an unfortunate occurrence.

Contact a reputable insurance company specializing in business insurance. Ask them to explain the various policies and limits of coverage available to you. Every state differs in its definition of liability. Get the facts.

Additional Insurance Coverage

Rules concerning worker's compensation differ from state to state. Worker's compensation insurance is required by law in the United States. It pays medical expenses and weekly income to employees who suffer job-related injuries. Call your insurance company or state department of labor for specific information pertaining to your state's requirements.

Owning and operating your own business dictates inescapable self-employment obligations necessitating careful consideration. One definite requirement is a personal health insurance policy. If you should hurt yourself on the job or perhaps get bitten by a dog, your health insurance policy will cover these expenses. Skyrocketing health costs can destroy the promising future of any business owner. Life insurance is another safeguard to contemplate.

Chapter 6

Choosing The Right Bank

You must open a separate business checking account. Take time and choose the most suitable bank for your banking needs. Converse with bank managers. Ask questions. List the advantages, disadvantages, and costs.

If this is your first experience opening a business account, find the expert. A customer service representative will be delighted to answer all of your inquiries. Some checking accounts require that you maintain a fixed monthly balance. Others may not. Some banks may also impose a monthly service charge. You will need to know these answers before selecting the bank for you.

It is to your advantage to choose a bank that is helpful to your business. The recommended banking services to suit your needs are usually available at either a small bank chain or an independent bank with no branches. In a small bank, your account may be very important. In a larger bank, you may not exist—you just blend in with the masses. In a smaller bank, the employees will become familiar with you and your business. This is extremely helpful if you intend to expand and apply for a loan. Your deposits will contain numerous personal checks and cash.

To open a business account, the bank will require precise information. Provide your Social Security number or federal identification number, driver's license and fictitious name registration certificate. If you have formed a corporation, bring the articles of incorporation and the corporate seal. This is proof of your corporate status. Also, bring along your occupational license. Make copies of all documents as you receive them. Save all paperwork for future reference.

Also remember, your bank can act as a reference to your customers and will be a credit reference for your suppliers. Start building credit right away. Don't wait until you need it.

Chapter 7

Pricing Your Services

You are a professional petsitter. You provide a specialized service to your customers and to their pets. You cannot duplicate or compare this service in any way to a kennel. Kennels charge between $5 and $12 per pet, per day and sometimes more. Their prices reflect daily rates. The pet owner pays according to the weight and size of each pet. There are specific criteria that all kennels require their customers to follow. Vaccinations must be current and inoculation documentation must accompany the pets. Pets must have a bath and flea dip before entering the boarding facility. The pets will spend *their* vacation time in a cage or a run. Pet owners must drop off and pick up their pets. Some kennels close on Sundays when most of their clientele return home from their trips. Pet owners must wait to pick up their pets on Monday.

Kennel cough, fleas and a host of contagious diseases may be prevalent in boarding facilities. This is understandable when a number of animals are together in close quarters. Some pets do fare well in a kennel environment, but most pet owners prefer an alternative.

Home-to-home petsitting is an excellent alternative! All our customers need to do is walk in their front door. Their happy and healthy pets are awaiting their arrival comfortably at home. Mail and newspapers are neatly stacked. Their home is spotlessly clean.

At first you may have to offer lower than normal rates to your initial customers. Before quoting any rates at all, set up your expense base. Develop a pricing scale that works for you. To turn a profit, your definitive goal, carefully assess all of your out-of-pocket expenses. Car and business insurance will be your major expenses. Estimate yearly gas consumption. Compute yearly advertising costs, office supplies, cleaning supplies, phone charges, employee wages, and licenses. Include all other costs you may incur that will be permanent, recurring expenses.

Calculate the total sum of these expenses to derive your yearly expense figure. Divide that figure by 12 months. This provides your monthly expenses. To derive your weekly expenses, divide the yearly expense figure by 52 (weeks). Divide that figure by 40, a typical work week, to determine your fixed hourly overhead expense. This is the cost per hour you spend to operate your business. Now you can structure your prices accordingly.

My prices were between $10 and $15 per visit. I charged $10 per visit for one to two cats located close to my home. I charged $15 to those with two or more pets who lived farther away. The duration of the visit should be no more than 45 minutes including traveling time. Charge more to customers who live greater distances. I gave deals (price breaks) to those who required multiple visits per day. I did the same for those who intended to be away for extended intervals.

Negotiate with your customers. Every circumstance is unique. It does not matter how many pets there are in the household to care for. **You do not charge by the pet. You are not a kennel.** Please use common sense and charge more when you must. **Your selling point for potential customers is that your set charge per visit is for their entire family of pets. Stress how much money you will be saving them !!!**

Do not over schedule yourself when doing your daily petsittings. To keep your gas expenses down, you must take a resourceful approach to traveling. Strategically plan your trips. Chart your customers' time schedules according to their pets' needs. Some customers may need you four or five times per day for one household.

Enter mileage traveled on your Daily Log Sheets and record gas consumption. Keep accurate records for tax deduction purposes. Use Forms #31 and #32.

Additional charges are necessary if your customers want you to bathe their pets. I charged $10 per bath using their shampoo. Extensive brushing was an additional $5 per visit for long-haired dogs and cats. Transporting a pet to the veterinarian for a planned appointment is considered a petsitting visit. Emergencies are charged by the hour. Walking a dog during lunch hour for the working pet owner is $7 to $10 per walk (about 20 minutes).

Sample Estimated Business Expenses

	YEARLY	MONTHLY
Gasoline	$1,200.00	$100.00
Car Insurance	600.00	50.00
Business Liability Insurance	500.00	41.67
Dishonesty Bond	100.00	8.33
Office Supplies	180.00	15.00
Telephone	300.00	25.00
Advertising	300.00	25.00
Wages One part-time worker - 10 hours weekly at $5.00 per hour	2,400.00	200.00
Licenses and Permits	100.00	8.33
TOTAL	**$5,780.00**	**$ 481.66**

Chapter 8

Getting The Word Out

Your advertising goal is maximum returns at minimum costs. Advertising is a pivotal business function. It could very well determine the success or failure of your business. It does pays to advertise! Effective advertising will probably be your most compensatory expense. Do not go overboard. There are many versatile ways to market yourself without spending the exhorbitant fees associated with radio, television and other media.

Classified Advertising

Your local newspaper is an excellent medium that is frequently used by the small advertiser. Classified ads are the most profitable means of advertising; they are extremely economical and cost effective. Classified ads are grouped by subject. When someone reads the classified ads, they look under specific headings for the product or services they need. You have already singled out your customers! Unlike the display ad which is randomly read, your classified ad is more targeted to those you want to reach. Small classified advertisements will suffice for the first year. Keep wording to a minimum. What you say is more important than how you say it. There is no need to be ostentatious or flamboyant. Be concise and to the point.

A common mistake is not advertising frequently enough. At first, run your classified ad consecutively for one month. Measure the effectiveness of the newspaper(s) you have chosen. The more frequently your ad appears, the more familiar the public will become with you. The more they see you, the better. Your ad will no doubt stand out amongst the other business services because it is unique. You will be noticed, I guarantee it. Your most productive months for advertising are April through December. Always remember to place an ad one month before all holidays.

Sample Classified Ads:

Personally Visit Veterinarians

Personally visit veterinarians in their offices, even though they may do boarding and you may be their competition. During the holiday season, their kennels may become overcrowded. Most vets will be happy to refer you to their customers to handle their overflow. You will also find that veterinarians will refer you to their customers with older pets. These pets often have medical problems and might not fare well in a kennel. They require tender, loving care that only a petsitting service can provide.

While making my rounds to veterinarians, I made friends with the technicians and receptionists. They were very obliging about accepting my brochures, cards and references. Word of mouth will be your most flattering form of advertising. Satisfied customers will rave about you to their friends.

Begin with your own veterinarian. Explain that you are starting a petsitting service in the area and request permission to use them as a reference. Gather a list of friends, colleagues, relatives, and those who can attest to your honesty and integrity. Ask their permission to use them as character references and to give out their phone numbers to potential clients. Advise them that this will be temporary. You will soon have a customer list a mile long with crowds of satisfied pet owners. Pet owners will ask you if they can be a reference! Just follow the instructions my manual provides, be very conscientious, and you will realize your aspirations.

Display Advertising

A display ad is invariably more expensive. It is larger than the classified ad and commonly appears with a border around the copy. This ad is normally found within the body of the newspaper. You may run the ad as many days as you desire or until your money runs out. Many publications will design the ad for you at no additional charge. I do not advise this mode of advertising unless you have a large advertising budget. If you do opt for this, make sure it's paying off by asking new customers how they heard about you.

Sample Display Advertisement

PET SITTING SERVICES

THERE'S NO PLACE LIKE HOME!

YOUR COMPLETE
PERSONAL PET
AND HOME CARE SERVICE

"WE SPECIALIZE IN T.L.C."

Licensed - Bonded - Insured

EXCELLENT REFERENCES

832-2899

Brochures

Another advertising vehicle to introduce your services is a brochure. Consider creating it as a self-mailer, which will save you on postage and envelope costs. The color of the brochure should be consistent with your business cards, letterheads and any correspondence you plan to use. You will find a sample brochure included with the business forms. It provides the necessary format to set up your own brochure. List the services you plan to offer. If the cost of brochures exceeds your budget, simply pass out modest flyers with the business name, phone number, and services. Post these flyers on apartment and community bulletin boards. Mail them to condominium associations. Do not deposit any literature into personal home or apartment mailboxes—that is against the law. Do not put flyers or brochures on the windshields of cars. Wind tends to be your enemy and you are basically littering parking lots. As you build up your clientele and spending capital, a brochure will be an essential advertising medium.

Unadorned brochures printed at a minimal price are available. One hundred brochures, 8-1/2" x 11", both sides printed and folded, cost about $30. Business cards are essential. You can buy 100 business cards for around $10. These two items, business cards and brochures, will be your golden tools of advertising.

Sample Brochure

PET SITTING SERVICES
P.O. BOX 563
ANYWHERE, FL 33440

Introducing You and Your Neighbors to Pet Sitting Services

A unique pet and home care service designed exclusively to give you peace of mind, and allow your pet or pets the luxury and security of remaining at home while you are away.

What we have to offer cannot be found in any kennel or boarding facility. We take pride in providing the utmost in the care and comfort of your pet and the general upkeep and maintenance of your home or condominium.

PET SITTING SERVICES is licensed, bonded and insured, serving our customers in the Broward and Palm Beach County areas. We have experience in all phases of pet care from pet grooming to pet shops.

As pet owners ourselves, we know the deep concern that goes along with leaving our pets behind, and **PET SITTING SERVICES** will help alleviate these worries and doubts. After all, our pets are a part of the family, too!!

For further information and a confidential interview, please call Pat or Alice Doyle, 555-0002 days, and 555-5000 evenings and weekends.

Yellow Pages Advertising

Advertising in the Yellow Pages of your telephone directory can triple your customer base. To be a Yellow Pages business advertiser, you must possess a business telephone line. This mandates the posting of an additional deposit to convert your residential telephone to a business telephone. Contact your local phone company for more information.

Prices for Yellow Page advertising can be astronomical. Start small and grow as your business expands. My ad was small but I received numerous calls. My listing displayed the business name and phone number. The classifications I chose to advertise under were Sitting Services and Pet Services. I signed a yearly contract and paid $30 per month for 12 months of Yellow Pages advertising. I never spent any more than that in all five years of petsitting. You may notice that your competitors have placed sizable advertisements. The prices for those large advertisements range from $100 a month and up. There is no reason to overspend in this mode of advertising. Companies who place large advertisements will not last long. Their overhead expenditures will eat up their profits. Again, common sense will help guide you.

Join Business Organizations

Join your local Chamber of Commerce. List yourself among the business services in your area. If an individual requests a petsitter, you'll be the one referred! Join the Better Business Bureau and Welcome Wagon in your area. Mingle with fellow business professionals in the neighborhood. The Better Business Bureau will provide you with the emblem of the BBB when you join. Proudly display this symbol to prospective clients and veterinarians.

Support Charities

Your altruistic spirit will reflect your business's reliability. Join your local humane society or the pet aid league. If you can, contribute to charities affiliated with animal welfare. Support national organizations and associations catering to animal well-being and participate in local fund raisers when possible. Here are some suggestions:

1. **Humane Society of the United States**
    2100 L Street, NW
    Washington, D.C. 20037
    (202)452-1100

Committed to providing food and shelter to homeless pets in the U.S. and various help programs.

2. **American Society for the Prevention of Cruelty to Animals**
    441 E. 92nd Street
    New York, New York 10128
    (212)876-7700

The first humane society in America. Provides information about the prevention of cruelty to animals throughout the U.S.

3.   **Massachusetts Society for the Prevention of Cruelty to Animals**
     350 South Huntington Avenue
     Boston, Massachusetts 02130

Founded in 1863, its mission is to protect animals, relieve their suffering, advance their welfare, prevent cruelty and work for a just and compassionate society.

4.   **Animal Welfare Institute**
     P.O. Box 3650
     Washington, D.C. 20007

Provides help, education and guidance to teach people to act with kindness, respect and responsibility toward all living things.

5.   **National Humane Education Society**
     15B Catoctin Circle S.E. #207
     Leesburg, VA 22075
     (703)777-8319

Dedicated to educating society on many positions dealing with the ethical and humane treatment of animals and their many contributions to all of us.

6.   **Friends of Animals**
     P.O. Box 1244
     Norwalk, CT 06856
     (203)866-5223

Devoted to saving endangered species by educating us as to the benefits they offer to society and nature.

7.   **The Delta Society**
     P.O. Box 1080
     Renton, WA 98057
     (206)226-7357

An organization dedicated to bringing pets and people together for companionship and therapy.

8.   **National Wildlife Federation**
     1400 Sixteenth Street, N.W.
     Washington, D.C. 20078-6420

Founded in 1936, the nation's largest, private, nonprofit conservation education program.

Also, send information on your business to these groups with your contribution.

Call On Local Businesses

Call on pet stores, grooming parlors and travel agencies. Distribute your brochures and references. Request permission to display them in their stores. Most small businesses will be happy to pass the word around. You can do the same for them. Reciprocation works wonders! Chances are your fellow small business owners will be supporters and recommend you to their customers.

Free Publicity

Prepare skillfully-written press releases or news releases. Mail them to local newspapers and magazines. The editor who reads them will be looking for a lively, interesting story and will print your business announcement free of charge under their new business services heading. They may pursue **you** for a newspaper article. You are a human interest story!

Sample Press Releases

DATE: May 10, 1991

To: Editor of *Sunshine News*

From: Petcare Services, Inc., 111 Elm Street, Jupiter, Fl 33445

Re: The announcement of a unique service business benefitting Palm Beach County and surrounding areas. Petcare Services is an in Home Pet Care and House Watching Service. Our purpose is to provide Tender Loving Care to your pets!

Dear Editor:

I would like to introduce my new service business to you and your readers. I started my business on May 1, 1991 and it is growing rapidly. It is a much needed service geared toward concerned pet owners. I feel that my business is truly unusual and warrants public attention! It is a definite human interest story! We are an invaluable asset to the traveling pet owner and home owner!! Please find the enclosed information and references on my company. We are licensed, bonded, insured, and a member of the Better Business Bureau. If you have any questions, please call me.

* NOTE: If you are advertising in their specific newspaper, TELL THEM.

Sincerely,

YOUR NAME AND POSITION: OWNER, PRESIDENT...ETC.

March 10, 1987

Palm Beach Post
2325 South Federal Highway
Delray Beach, FL 3445

Dear Sir/Madam:

I have a four-year-old [or new if you are just getting started] UNIQUE service business that I think might be of interest to you and your readers.

I have enclosed some photographs and newspaper articles as well as my brochure and references to help familiarize you with our concept.

Although we are based in _____, we have recently expanded as far south as _____ and as far north as _____.

I'm sure you'll feel as I do that our concept is both newsworthy and noteworthy. Please contact me for further information!

Sincerely,

_____

Mail these press releases to newspapers in the areas where you plan to offer your services, no matter how big or small. Many newspapers contacted me and took my picture with a collection of pets. They provided me with lots of free coverage and publicity!! Reporters actually drove around with me on my pet visits. (Of course, I had permission from the pet owners.) They wrote glowing articles about my business. They personally experienced the hands-on loving care involved in the petsitting service industry. The result: **free advertising** with a twist of a real life adventure for the journalist!

References

I have alluded continuously to **references** and their importance to your credibility, honesty and legitimacy. Once you start your company, success depends on gaining satisfied customers who will tell others about your business. Virtually 90 percent of new business comes from referrals. Your customers will be entrusting you with the keys to their homes, their burglar alarm codes, and most crucial, their pets' lives. For these reasons, potential customers will definitely require a list of references from you. Personal recommendations from veterinarians and other pet care professionals are very significant.

Direct Mail Advertising

Another avenue for promoting your business is through direct mail advertising. This is the mailing of information directly into the homes of prospective clients. Mailing lists are available to the public and help pinpoint primary goals. Purchase lists containing names of those you specifically want to reach, pet owners. This saves time, stamps, and wasted literature on those who will never respond.

Compilations of mailing lists are available at your local county animal care and control division. They compile the names and addresses of both dog and cat owners in the county where you request the information. There are also mailing list companies who specialize in this field. The animal care and control division and mailing list companies charge by the name. My suggestion is to map out the territories closest to you.

If you plan to mail large quantities of letters, call your local post office to get bulk mailing rates. Prices are quite favorable for large volumes of mail, but there is an initial fee as well as a yearly permit fee.

Specialty Advertising

Depending on the amount of money you allot to your advertising budget, specialty advertising is another effective method to gain recognition. Any items brandishing your business name are prominent advertising tools and make excellent giveaway items. Key chains, litter box scoopers, bagged doggy and kitty treats, refrigerator magnets with your name, phone number and logo are some examples. These are practical and useful items for your customers. You can find the names of companies that sell promotional items in the Yellow Pages.

Speaking Engagements

Consider speaking engagements at regional men's and women's organizations and schools. Contact your local talk radio station and suggest a question and answer interview with the talk host. Respond to questions from the community about your business.

Dog And Cat Shows

Check with pet organizations or refer to national pet magazines for details on trade shows or pet shows. At these exhibitions, you can rent a booth and gain some high profile visibility. Many cat and dog shows hold spectacular events in local cities around the country. Pass out brochures and specialty items if you desire. Fashion your display in an eye-catching and appealing style. Write or call to find out whether these associations will sponsor shows in your area:

1.   **The American Kennel Club**
     51 Madison Avenue
     New York, New York 10010
     (212)696-8350

2.   **The Cat Fancier's Association, Inc.**
     1309 Allaire Avenue
     Ocean, New Jersey 07712
     (908)528-9797

Cable T.V. And Radio

Cable television companies have designated information channels where advertisements are viewed by their subscribers. Advertise directly into the living rooms of families you want to reach.

You can also buy time on the airwaves from a local AM or FM radio station but this method is quite costly. I suggest you put this idea on hold until you build up a little capital.

There are countless ways to advertise your services! But budget yourself carefully, then test and track the results of each method. Stick with the ones that pay off. There is no reason to go overboard. Your reputation will be your most convincing means for public awareness.

Chapter 9

Accounting and Bookkeeping

Unsatisfactory planning and careless recordkeeping are two primary causes for countless small business failures. Map out your strategy. Organization requires self-discipline. Too many owners of small companies place the accounting process low on their list of priorities.

Nothing makes more sense than to supervise the direction of your business. Bookkeeping methods must be consistent. Records must be accurate and comprehensive. The law requires you to save all books and records of your business transactions and have them available for inspection. Proper management and meticulous recordkeeping are essential to running a smooth and successful operation.

Assign each customer an identification number. Starting with your very first customer, their assigned account number will be #1. This number must appear on all associated documents involving this customer. This number is on the key tag that holds the customer's house keys. Do not write the customer's name or address on the key tag. If you were to lose those keys, the person who finds the keys will know exactly whose they are. All they would need to do is look up the name in the telephone book and get the address. The keys to the front door, handed right over to them by their friendly petsitting service! This is a nightmare you do not want to go through. We will discuss the safety precautions you need to take in the chapters ahead.

Set up individual ledger sheets on each customer. A ledger is a book in which business transactions are recorded in chronological order. Include their name, address, phone number and customer identification number. Document all invoice charges and payments here.

Your checking account may double as your income and expense ledger. On every check stub, write to whom and what you are paying for. Log all bank deposits. Bank deposits are your income and checks disbursed are your business expenses.

All invoice charges and payments must be kept up-to-date for accurate billing determinations. A more detailed accounting procedure may be necessary in the future. For now, a simplistic method will allow you more time to devote to building your business.

Keep an accurate record of your receivables (invoices) on the Accounts Receivable Log, (Form #29). Receivables are monies owed to you from your customers. Save all sales receipts associated with anything you purchase for the business. Gas receipts, telephone bills, etc., are business deductions if used for the business only. Pay all bills by check to document business expenses accurately.

Record daily mileage. You must maintain contemporaneous records of automobile and entertainment expenses. Consult a certified public accountant for details on permissible tax deductions, tax advantages and the preparation of tax returns. A qualified accountant will play a very significant role in your business. His or her advice will have the highest impact on your financial strategy and will help steer you in the right direction.

Local stationery and office supply stores carry simplified monthly bookkeeping journals. These books contain the forms suitable for recording the outcome of one year's business transactions. Monthly and annual summary sheets of income and expenses are available. If hiring helpers, weekly payroll and employee earnings records are available.

Taxes and the Business Owner

You are considered self employed if you are a sole proprietor, a corporation, or a partnership. Therefore, you are responsible for estimated federal income taxes. These taxes are by law due on a quarterly basis and are filed as follows: April 15, June 15, September 15 and January 15. This schedule must be followed strictly as to avoid any penalties that you may owe to the IRS because you did not pay enough income tax when it was due. This also helps to manage your money so at the end of the year one entire lump sum is not due all at once. Your estimated federal income tax payments include your Social Security taxes owed. Consult your accountant on how to figure your estimated taxes.

Taxes and the Business Use of Your Car

You are able to deduct business-related car expenses on your income tax returns if you are operating your car, truck or van for business purposes. You must follow specific guidelines issued by the Internal Revenue Service. You must maintain accurate records to show business use. If you drive your car for both business and personal uses, you must separate your expenses between business and personal.

There are two alternatives from which to choose when deducting car expenses. You may deduct car expenses by claiming the standard mileage rate or by using actual expenses such as gasoline, car repairs, insurance, etc. If you maintain precise records of your daily mileage, you may opt to use the standard mileage rate. This means that you can take the standard mileage rate of .28 cents per mile for every mile you have recorded over the course of the year. However, if you choose the standard mileage rate method, you cannot deduct expenses such as depreciation, maintenance, repairs, gasoline, oil, car insurance and vehicle registration fees. If you choose to use the standard mileage rate, you must choose to use it in the very first year you begin operating your business.

Your second option is to deduct your actual car expenses. You must choose which method gives you the largest deduction. The following items are actual car expenses: tolls and parking fees, gasoline, oil, repairs, garage rent, insurance, lease fees, rental fees, licenses and depreciation of your vehicle.

If your car is damaged, destroyed or stolen, you may be able to deduct part of the loss that is not covered by insurance. For more information on this subject, call the IRS at 1-800-TAX-FORM and ask for Publication #917, *Business Use of Your Car*.

Taxes and the Business Use of Your Home

If you use your home for business, you are able to deduct certain expenses for business use. However, you must meet certain requirements in order to be eligible for these deductions. If you use part of your home, you may deduct the following direct and indirect expenses: painting or repairs made to the specific area or room used for business, real estate taxes, mortgage interest, rent, utilities, security systems, casualty losses and depreciation. There is a percentage rate that is used to determine the amount of expenses you can deduct. More specific information can be found in the IRS Publication #587, *Business Use of Your Home*.

See the Appendix for the IRS information telephone number in your state.

Roadblocks That Lead To Business Failure

1. Inadequate planning

2. Poor recordkeeping

3. Neglecting duties

4. Incompetence

5. Disinterest

6. Lack of control in disbursing funds

Only you have control over success or failure.

A Quick Accounting Lesson

ASSETS: Those items of value owned by a business. Example: computer, office furniture, machinery, etc.

LIABILITIES: What the business owes its creditors.

OWNER'S EQUITY: Money the owner has invested in the business.

ASSETS MINUS LIABILITIES = OWNER'S INVESTMENT

ASSETS = LIABILITIES PLUS OWNER'S EQUITY

REVENUE: Income derived from services or sales

EXPENSES: Money spent for those items needed to run the business. In accounting terms, an outward flow of assets.

Invoicing And Payment

On your very last petsitting visit to the home, bring the invoice along with you. Prepare it ahead of time. Leave it for your customer along with a friendly note. Hand delivering the invoice saves on postage and prevents a backlog on billing. To assure prompt payment, imprint "DUE UPON RECEIPT" on all invoices. Keep a copy of the invoice and place it in the outstanding (unpaid) invoices file folder. Record all invoice amounts and payments on the customer ledger sheets and on the Accounts Receivable Log, Form #29.

You can expect to receive payment within one to three weeks. Expect payment in the form of a check or cash. When you receive the payment, remove the copy of the invoice from your outstanding invoice folder. Next, pull your customers's ledger sheet. Record the date you received the payment, amount and the check number. Mark the invoice "PAID" and place in the customer's file. Pull your accounts receivable log, indicate the paid invoice amount, and deduct that amount from your running total.

Deal with late payments in an appropriate and friendly manner (see Forms #33 and #34). A phone call or a reminder letter with a copy of the invoice is usually all that is necessary. Checks returned to you by the bank for insufficient funds should be addressed with a phone call and a follow-up letter (Form #35). Accept only cash, money orders or cashier's checks to replace the bad checks. Remember to collect the check charge the bank imposes on your account. If a customer is planning to be away for more than two weeks, request a 50 percent deposit.

Chapter 10

The Home Office

I n any successful business venture, an orderly method of operation leads you directly down the path to prosperity. Without an accurate plan of action, a business is at the mercy of fate, ruled by laws based on chance.

Building and managing your petsitting service requires logical determinations and strategic planning. Know what to expect in return, not only in dollars. Satisfaction is knowing you have created and chosen the proper course to follow.

Running the business from the comfort and privacy of your own home is not only convenient but cost effective. There is no need for the debt of an office setup. You can turn personal expenses such as rent, utilities, depreciation of your home, household suppliers, furniture, telephone bills, interest on your mortgage, repair of the office portion of the home, and much more into tax deductible items if they meet the IRS requirements.

First, you must determine if it is legal for you to work out of your home. In some states, zoning ordinances may prohibit you from using your home for business purposes. Also, check your condominium and homeowner's association rules and regulations. They may state in their by-laws that you may not run a business from your dwelling. In actuality, you are maintaining a home office and tending to your customers outside of your home rather than having customers come to you. Therefore, zoning ordinances should have no bearing on a service such as this. To find out about zoning ordinances, call your local city or state planning and zoning department.

Select a room or section of a room in your home. Privacy is essential. I suggest the following supplies to run an efficient office. A locking letter-size filing cabinet is necessary. This cabinet holds your customer information file and keys to your client's homes. No one but you may access the files. Keep the files under lock and key AT ALL TIMES! **Only YOU have authorization to peruse these confidential files!**

An easy way to proficiently track your petsitting appointments is to invest in a chalkboard or dry erase board. Here, on the wall of your office, you display daily, weekly and monthly assignments. Update the schedule daily.

On a personal note, it is very easy to get distracted while working from home. You must separate your personal life from your business life or your enterprise will suffer greatly. Set a daily goal. Write up a daily schedule for yourself, a sort of "to do" list that you will follow as a daily ritual. Aside from basic office supplies, you will need:

1. Desk or table

2. Telephone

3. Telephone answering machine

4. Appointment book and calendar

5. Letter-size or legal-size file folders

6. Letter-size or legal-size filing cabinet (locking)

7. Adding machine or calculator

8. Disposable key tags

9. Rubber stamp and ink pad with business name and address

10. Clasp envelopes, size 6 x 9. Attach to the inside cover of the file folders. This envelope is to hold the house keys. Place a strip of Velcro™ tape on the underside closing flap of the envelope. Place another piece of tape directly across from the other. This will secure the envelope opening. I suggest Velcro™ tape in place of using the aluminum clasp. Constantly opening and closing the key envelope wears out the clasp too quickly. We want to insure that the keys are safely secure within the envelope and unable to slip out.

11. Printed agreements and release forms (included with this manual)

12. Legal pads

13. Velcro™ tape

14. Mileage logbook

15. Typewriter or computer with pad or stand and ribbon

16. Business cards

17. Brochures

18. Letterheads

19. Legal-size envelopes

20. Fireproof security safe (optional)

21. Local area map

22. Veterinary first aid kit

23. Chalkboard or dry erase board

24. In and out boxes

25. Postage stamps or postage meter

26. Index cards

27. Glue

28. Computer diskettes

Chapter 11

The Telephone Call

Once you place your ad, inquiries will keep your phone lines buzzing. Pet owners are very enthusiastic when a loving alternative to a kennel appears. These initial calls are extremely important when introducing your new business. How you answer and what you answer is critical. Return all telephone calls promptly.

When a prospective client calls, respond in a congenial yet businesslike manner. Always answer with the name of your business and announce who you are. Record all information from the caller on the form I have provided titled the Customer Call-In Report (Form #3). Fill out a report on *every* inquiring customer. Place it in the inquiries file. It contains the date of the call, name, address, home and work phone numbers of the caller. It asks for the number and type of pet(s), dates and times needed. It also asks how they found out about you: your newspaper ad, your vet, or the chamber of commerce. Keep a record for effective advertising purposes. **Always get their telephone number if nothing else!!!** This allows you to follow up on your prospect.

Respond to inquiries promptly. Mail out an information package to *every* person who contacts you. This package should contain a brochure, business card and list of references. Compose a friendly personalized letter to arrange an informal, no charge, no obligation appointment. The initial interview is most important. You will be meeting with the owners and their pets before their departure date. Your objective is to have them hire you.

When you talk with a customer on the telephone, be consistent with your answers. Have a list of information and prices nearby for reference.

You must purchase a reliable answering machine! When you are not home to answer business calls, always engage your answering machine. There may be times when a customer has to leave town on an emergency. He or she may leave you a quick message on the recorder. The message may say that they must leave for a week and could you please care for his dog? He will assume that you have received the message. If you have an unreliable, dysfunctional machine, replace it with a new one. It could result in an unthinkable catastrophe. Buy a machine with the capabilities of call retrieval. This enables you to call from another telephone and retrieve your messages by simply pressing a secret code number.

Your recorded announcement (greeting) on your answering machine should be friendly and businesslike. Explain that you are not in at present but their call is very important to you. Ask them to please leave their name, number and a brief message. Be creative. Compose a refreshingly novel jingle. Return their call as soon as possible. Check your messages frequently from wherever you are. Several times a day. Response time is critical. Again, do not let too much time lapse before returning calls.

Another option to consider is to engage the help of a telephone answering service. There are live operator answering services and automatic voice mail services where your messages are electronically stored awaiting retrieval from a touch tone phone in a computer. Voice mailboxes are state-of-the-art answering machines used by countless business owners today. Voice mailboxes are inexpensive to rent and are available to receive messages 24 hours a day.

Your telephone company offers a myriad of features, many of which I suggest you add to your telephone system. Call waiting is a feature that allows another call to get through to you by alerting you with a click or a beep. This is very helpful because one thing callers do not want to hear is a busy signal. You can answer the other call by simply pushing a button, placing your first call on hold. This enables you to answer the awaiting customer. You can take their name and number and return their call as soon as you conclude your other call.

"Custom ringing" is another feature I suggest. If you do not have a separate business line and you are using your home phone to answer business calls, custom ringing allows you to have two telephone numbers on one telephone. You will have an additional telephone number added along with your regular home telephone number, which you can give out as your business phone number. You will have one line ringing within its regular interval of time in between rings. The second line will have two short rings. You will be able to distinguish a business call from a personal call from the number of rings you hear. Remember, you cannot advertise in the Yellow Pages with this option. Only with a separate business line may you do so.

Answering the Telephone Call

You must assimilate the following facts to competently answer the many questions that prospects will ask:

1. You run a professional pet and home care service business. You care for their pet(s) in their home. You do not take the pets into your home. You are bonded and insured. You are a member of the Better Business Bureau. You have excellent references. You hold a city and county occupational license. You make daily and nightly home visits. You spend about 45 minutes per visit, which provides ample time for feeding, walking, playing, and cuddling.

2. Emphasize to the prospective client that home-to-home petsitting offers them freedom and peace of mind. They may never have had this convenience before. Your competent service allows their pets to remain in their own comfortable and familiar surroundings. Their pets' regular routines remain virtually unchanged. You also meticulously care for their home.

3. Your primary function is to accommodate their pets in every way possible. You attend to all special dietary needs and feeding times. You provide clean, fresh water and food daily. You scoop and change the litter box, clean bird cages, administer medication, and perform basic grooming requirements.

4. You will visit dogs no less than twice per day. Once in the morning and again in the evening. Space visits no more than 12 hours apart. When walking a dog, always use a leash! No exceptions! The owner will instruct you where to walk the dog, for how long, and if you need a pooper scooper.

5. You will visit cats once per day unless the owner stipulates additional visits. Times will vary and you will find that caring for cats allows you more flexibility in scheduling your visits. Always enter the house with your hands covering the bottom open area of the open door. Cats are quick and can dart out between your legs.

6. If you notice any change in behavior, such as poor eating habits or lethargy, you will take the pet to their veterinarian without delay.

7. In addition to pet care, you also provide home services at no additional charge. These tasks include mail collection, newspaper pick up, and plant care. You will start their car daily for battery maintenance purposes, do general cleanup and garbage removal. You will maintain adequate lighting in the evenings to help burglar-proof their home. You will open and close their curtains and blinds for added security purposes. You will make sure all windows and doors remain locked and secured on every visit.

8. Inquire as to their traveling plans. Suggest they set up an appointment to meet with you. Request a date and time convenient for all to gather. Get directions to their home. Call an hour before the interview to confirm your appointment and to let them know you are coming.

9. Discuss prices at the close of the telephone call if at all possible. If you are going to offer overnight stays (sleep overs), the hours for this exclusive service is 9:00 P.M. to 8:00 A.M. I charged $35 to $40 per night.

10. Punctuality is foremost. There is no substitute for conscientious, detailed reliability. Stress your dedication to your profession.

11. Your clients will question you about employees. Contrary to popular belief, it is prudent to hire people you know personally, perhaps a friend or a family member. Reassure the client that they will meet the person who will be caring for their pets and home. Explain the rigorous training that accompanies the hiring of a helper. Reiterate the rules concerning confidentiality.

12. There is an inevitable amount of rejection that goes along with this business. Unfortunately, we live in a skeptical society. The public views humanity with pessimism rather than with optimism. Don't take disapproval to heart.

13. Some people will compare your prices to kennels and may believe your prices are out of line. Quality care is not their concern. They are just looking for a bargain. You are their most priceless bargain!

14. Demeaning the competition is bad business. To put down another's business for your own self gain is immature and unprofessional. You will achieve respect from customers by the loving care you provide their pets. Competition is the life of trade. All businesses must do their utmost to keep customers and gain new ones.

Immediately write all appointments and petsitting schedules in your appointment book.

Chapter 12

The Initial Interview

The first meeting between you and the pet's owners will be the determining factor on whether or not you have the job. The petsitting profession places you on a more personal level with your clients. The first and foremost responsibility we assume when caring for pets is their physical needs: nourishment, adequate living conditions, and health care. This also includes grooming and exercise. The next area of responsibility demands emotional support and attention. An animal is very dependent upon humans for affection, and company. Third, an obligation to secure the home and keep it neat and orderly is an essential requirement. The above facts must be convincingly relayed to the pet owners during the initial interview.

You know the old saying about first impressions? It could never be more true. You must project a personal yet professional persona every time you meet with a new customer.

Consider every meeting as a job interview. Dress in a comfortable, appropriate manner. Carry a briefcase or a file holder to transport your paperwork. Acknowledge the owners and greet the pets with enthusiasm. Ask their pets' names. While conversing, recount the details of your initial telephone conversation. This will impress your client. The owners closely monitor your interactions with their pets. Give them your undivided attention. They will recognize the warmth and dedication you exude by the attention you display to their pets.

Bring an information package along with you in case the owners did not receive one before the meeting. The purpose of this gathering is to get to know one another, the pets, and the household routine. Instill confidence within them so they feel comfortable leaving their pet and home in your care.

Your next step is to suggest that everyone sit down together and go over all details of the pet sit. Place a copy of your business license, insurance and bonding information, proof of membership in the Chamber of Commerce, the Better Business Bureau and local Humane Society into a loose leaf binder. Hold a mini presentation of your business and the services you provide. Shortly after my business started, I placed pictures of my customers' pets in my binder. The pet owners loved it! While they are browsing through your binder, explain all that you will do.

A copy of your membership sticker should be placed in your intial interview binder along with you business license and proof of insurance and/or bonding.

Introduce the contents of their private customer file. Explain how they are now a confidential customer account number. Their name coincides directly with their assigned customer account number. This number is used on all correspondence dealing with this specific customer. Their house key is placed on a key tag exhibiting this number. Again, if the keys are misplaced or lost, the person finding the key will not have any information about where this key belongs. A definite securtity safeguard. Suggest they provide their neighbors or friends with an extra set of house keys.

It is now time to fill out the customer file. Always prepare the customer file before the initial interview. Fill in names, addresses, and phone numbers before the meeting. Do not do this during the interview. It is too time consuming and you need to be interacting on a personal level at this time. The customer file includes several forms that contain essential information on your customers and pets. Most forms require signatures.

Attached to the inside flap of the file folder is a clasp envelope to hold the house key(s). Place a numbered key tag inside the envelope for you to place the keys on. Do this also before the meeting. The General Information Sheet and Pet Data Information Sheet, Forms #10 and #14, contains the customer's name, address, home and work phone numbers. These forms list the out-of-town phone numbers, emergency numbers, information about feeding and visitation schedules. They provide the garbage days, newspaper pickup, mail collection, plant watering instructions, medical problems, medications, and more.

When you have finished filling out all applicable forms, you should not have one question about what to do or where to find anything. The customer file will be your bible on each pet.

Also contained in the customer file will be the Release of Liability forms (Forms #6 and #7). These forms hold you harmless from any culpability while the pets are alone in the home and when others such as friends or family members, the pest control company, contractors or anyone who has access to the home at the same time you do. The Medical Emergency Release form, #16, assigns you the authority to take their pet to their veterinarian or emergency veterinarian in case of illness. Use the Burglar Alarm Information Sheet (Form #13) when a security system is present in the home.

Most customers prefer you hold a set of their house keys on file. That is an excellent idea. You don't have to make a special trip to pick up their keys each time they go away. In this case, they will need to sign the Release for Key on File, Form #11. This document assigns permission to retain a customer's keys on file in a locking cabinet or safe. Only you will have access to it.

I suggest filling out the General Information Sheet last. You must accompany the owner and walk through the house, writing information as you go. You will be shown the kitchen, the pet's feeding area, location of the kitty litter, where to dispose of the cat litter scoopings, location of the food, litter, cleaning supplies, where they prefer the dog to be walked, etc.

Upon receiving the keys to the home, immediately place them on their key tag. Put the keys back into the clasp envelope and secure tightly. Assure your clients that their pets will be in safe and caring hands. If they wish, they may call you to check in and see that all is well. Ask them to please call you when they return home from their trip. Suggest they leave a message on your recorder to alert you that they have arrived home safely. We all know how famous the airlines are at running late or there may be other reasons why your clients may not have made it home on time. If they are delayed, you **must** make another trip especially if you are caring for a dog.

Hired and ready to go—99.9 percent of the times you enter the home of a prospective client for an initial interview, you've got the job! Follow my steps and you will every time. Remember to post every custome's schedule in your daily appointment book as soon as you have the schedule.

Do not over schedule yourself. On some occasions, you will have early morning sittings and the rest of the day free. If you are booked to the maximum capacity you know you can handle efficiently, do not accept additional sitting appointments. Allow yourself enough time between sittings to gather your thoughts and to rest. Petsitter exhaustion is not an uncommon phenomenon. The ones who will suffer most are the pets, and they must be your first and foremost consideration.

Realistically, if you are handling all the petsitting alone, you can petsit four dogs per day. With one helper, you can care for eight dogs per day. Dogs must be walked once in the morning and once at night. This means that you must schedule yourself for two visits per dog per day, scheduling each walk approximately 12 hours apart. Some customers will break up the day with three visits and specify the time of each visit. You must adjust your schedule accordingly. Your first visit should begin at 5:30 A.M. and your last visit to your last dog on the schedule should begin no later than 9:00 A.M. Evening visits must begin again at 5:30 P.M. and follow the same time sequence as the morning scheduled walks. Throughout the day you have seven hours in which to schedule mid-day walks, cat visits, horse checkups or go to your home office to return phone calls or prepare your schedule for the next day.

Generally, cats have no synchronized time schedules unless medication is to be administered at prescribed intervals or if an owner requests specific times. You can safely schedule 15 cat sittings per day. You can see the advantage of hiring a helper as it doubles your petsitting power and gives you the option to take on more clients each day to boost your daily income.

Use The Following Forms In The Customer File

Form #13: Burglar Alarm Information Sheet

Form #10: General Information Sheet

Forms #17, 18, 19: Housewatching Forms (homes only)

Form #30: Invoice

Form #15: Medication Instruction Sheet (used for sick pets only)

Form #8:   Natural Disaster Instruction Sheet

Form #14: Pet Data and Information Sheet

Form #12: Postal Release (if owners require signature for mail)

Form #6:   General Release Form and Disclaimer of Liability*

Form #11: Release for Key on File (only to retain keys on file)

Form #16: Veterinarian Medical Emergency Release Form

* Limits of liability are specifically defined in every state. I strongly urge you to contact an attorney to review all business forms provided.

Chapter 13

Personal Safety

You will be making your livelihood through your car. It is extremely important that you have dependable, reliable transportation.

You alone are responsible for the well-being and proper care of these pets. They depend on you to be there.

Routinely inspect all fluid levels of your car. Check the oil, transmission fluid, brake fluid, water and antifreeze in your radiator. Change the oil regularly. Tune up the car at regular intervals. Add water to your battery if needed. Carry jumper cables with you. Keep the gas tank full. Be sure the tires are in good condition. Check the air pressure in your tires. Always have a spare in the trunk and know how to change your own tire. Carry a flashlight and use it when you are walking dogs in the evening. I carried a small can of mace and a whistle on my key ring for extra protection.

Each time you arrive at a client's home, be observant enough to know if something is awry. Keep you eyes and ears open. If you observe a window open or a door ajar or unlocked, immediately drive away! Call the police from the nearest phone. **Do not enter the home.** Do not open the door to strangers. Request that the owners supply a list of real estate associates (if the home is for sale), repairmen, lawn maintenance workers, exterminators, or anyone who will be entering the home during the same time period you are caring for their pets. This includes family members and neighbors. Form #7, General Release Form, fulfills these requirements.

Take added precautions. Always lock your car. If you are transporting additional customer files in the car with you, lock them in your trunk. **Never** set customer files on the front or back car seat or where they are readily visible and accessible to anyone with dubious intentions. Have the key to the house out and ready to use. Lock the door immediately behind you. Keep the house key on your person the entire visit. Place the keys in your pocket or affix them to your belt. Make this a habit to prevent locking yourself out. I locked myself out of a home with eight cats. It was my very first petsitting job. Imagine the panic! As the door shut behind me, I knew I had done it. My heart sank. But, I did not panic. I kept a cool head. Fortunately, the windows in the house were open and I removed the screen from the front window. I crawled through carefully, making sure that none of the cats I was sitting escaped. There they were, sitting in a semicircle watching me fly head first into the living room! I made a fool of myself as eight cats looked on. I learned my lesson from that experience. I was lucky that time, but from then on I made sure that would never happen to me again. Since then, I immediately placed the keys to each home in my pocket after unlocking the door.

It has always been my position that late night visits be performed only when *absolutely* necessary. I advise your policy reflect the last visit to be no later than 9:00 P.M. Although there is safety in numbers, remember, it is not a good idea to bring friends or family members into the homes where you are caring for pets. Your bond and insurance will not cover any damages or accusations of theft if something happens. Allow them to ride along with you but ask them to please wait in the car.

Do not place magnetic signs on your car when performing your petsittings. By doing this, you are advertising that the owners are out of town.

Do not wear a T-shirt or sweatshirt bearing the name of your company when performing your petsittings. This also advertises the fact that no one is home.

Always leave a travel plan at home with your family. Let them know exactly where your schedule leads you and what time you will be home. If you are running late, call and let someone know when you plan to arrive.

Animal Bites: If you are bitten by a pet, do the following: Clean the wound and determine the extent of the injury. The bite may not be evidenced beyond a bruise or a scratch on the skin. If the wound appears to be deep, or if suturing is necessary, go to the nearest hospital emergency room.

The National Safety Council is the world's largest safety organization serving America. They cover all aspects of safety practices and procedures. Write or call for your free business manual specifically targeting small business owners: National Safety Council, 444 North Michigan Avenue, Chicago, IL 60611, (800)621-7619.

Chapter 14

A Quick Review and the Actual Petsit

The lingering dilemma of what to do with Fido and Felix while on vacation no longer exists. Pet owners no longer need to rush home on a lunch hour to walk their dog. No more worrying about what to do with their pet if they want to sneak away for a weekend getaway.

The true selling point of a petsitting service is elementary. The pets remain comfortably at home while the owners are away. Petsitters make daily and nightly visits to the pets, substituting for pet owners. Petsitters care for the pets personally and professionally. Petsitters also bill themselves as a home care service as well as a pet care service.

The following is an informative review of the services that you will be performing on your day-to-day petsitting service schedule:

1. You have already met with the owners of the pet(s) you will be caring for. Familiarize yourself with the data in their file. The signed documents and essential paperwork contained within the customer file are in your possession. The General Information Sheet provides the dates and times to perform your services. It contains specific instructions from the owners. It also holds the key(s) to the house. Carry the customer file with you on every visit to ensure accurate and precise execution of all instructions.

2. Pick up the newspapers and mail upon arrival. Be sure all doors, gates and windows remain locked. Check the perimeter of fenced-in areas to ensure no holes were dug that pets could escape through. If you find any, thoroughly fill the holes and fortify the area with a concrete block or piece of wood. Enter the home. Lock the door behind you. Once inside, arrange the mail in a neat pile on the kitchen table or wherever the owner has stipulated. Set the garbage out on specified days of the week. Always carry in the receptacles after garbage pickups.

3. In some cases you will have a burglar alarm code. The code is typically a four-digit series of numbers and has a 15-second delay. This enables you enough time to press in the code and disarm the alarm. Find these directions on the Burglar Alarm Information Sheet. Check the file before entering a home.

4. Affectionately greet the pets!! I am sure they will have already met you cheerfully at the door. If you are caring for dogs, whisk them out for a walk without delay. Walk only in areas designated by the owner. Some communities or homeowner's associations have ordinances or regulations that require you to remove dog feces from public view. Some states have adopted and strictly enforce laws of this nature. You could pay a hefty fine if you do not adhere to these regulations. You must buy a "pooper scooper." Your local pet shop carries them. Take the dog on a vigorous walk and give him plenty of exercise. When walking a dog and you observe an unleashed dog in the vicinity, avert a confrontation. Return to the home at once.

    Although you have previously met the pets you will be caring for, there may be occasions where a fair amount of time has passed since the initial interview and a dog may forget who you are and mistake you for a stranger. The dog may exhibit either aggressive or passive behavior in this scenario. Overly aggressive dogs usually bark continuously and not allow you to enter the premises. If the dog is skittish and retreats to a bedroom or part of the house to hide, you will have to seek him or her out. The best advice I can give you is to acknowledge your situation. Enter the home by slowly opening the front door and calling the dog's name. Hearing his or her name assures the dog that you know him or her and they should know you. Let the dog come to you. If the dog will not let you enter, get out your supply of dog biscuits and bribe your way inside. If a dog is timid and reluctant to respond to your commands, be patient and calm. They are just afraid. Don't forget that this may be the first time they have been left alone. Call their name softly and do not raise your voice or make any sudden movements. Eventually, they will feel more at ease. This situation does not occur often. During the initial interview, you should try to ascertain if the dog is vicious or shy. Do not accept the petsitting job if you feel uneasy with the pet.

    There may be occasions when you will be caring for two or more dogs in one household. A dog fight may break out. Do not try to separate the dogs with your bare hands. You will surely get bitten. The most common way diseases are transmitted from pets is through animal bites. Get a large glass of water from the kitchen and throw it on them. It works like a charm every time. Put the dogs in separate rooms for a while. They will be alright once they calm down. Jealousy is usually the culprit.

5. If you are caring for a cat(s), be sure all are present in the house. They love to hide in unusual places. Locate them to assure yourself they are all right. Always account for all pets. Follow feeding instructions. Change the water daily. Scoop the litter and change it when necessary. Flush the scoopings down the toilet or place into a plastic bag and seal securely for proper sanitary disposal. Ask the owners what they prefer.

    Cats are complex little characters. They are independent and self-reliant. Most cats are friendly and loving, but there are a chosen few who let you know who is boss. If a cat does not want to be stroked or held, do not persist. If a cat does not want the attention, there is no way you can force him or her to accept it. Give up and move on to another pet. Some customers who know the behavior of their cats will instruct you to come into their home, check to see that the cats are all accounted for, scoop the litter box, leave fresh food and water and go on your way. I prefer to stay and give the cats lots of love and affection. That's the proper way to petsit.

6. Some pet owners may ask you to brush or comb their cat or dog. This is usually an easy task. Most pets love to be brushed. It's a superb way of giving attention!

7. Birds must have their water and food changed daily. You will care for your share of exotic birds from parakeets to toucans. A basic diet consists of fresh vegetables and fruit together with seed and other basic nutritional foods according to the owner's instructions.

8. You will care for freshwater fish as well as saltwater fish. Saltwater tanks need a little more attention than do freshwater tanks. Your main role will be to feed the fish. Turn on and off the aquarium lights and enjoy the beautiful species of fish. Do not overfeed. If you notice any cloudiness in the water or if a fish looks ill, call your local pet shop. Find one that specializes in tropical fish. You may have to bring in a water sample from the tank. They will analyze it for you to determine the problem, and they will prescribe the remedy. There may be occasions when you will have to spend your own money. Save the receipt, and add the amount to your client's invoice.

9. Plant care is another service we provide. Rule of green thumb as I have learned: It is better to under water than to over water. Pinpoint each plant and obtain proper watering and placement instructions.

10. General cleanup is basic. Recycle all pet food cans and throw trash away. Wash all dishes and utensils for use on your next visit. Take out the garbage. Sweep the floors or vacuum the carpeting. From time to time, accidents do occur. Fido just couldn't hold it until you got there. Please expect these mistakes to occur. Clean the areas thoroughly with a disinfectant cleanser. Do not punish or reprimand a pet for accidents such as these or for any reason. It is a part of our job. Patience and understanding are the very core of our profession.

11. Always be on time. Your customers and their pets depend upon your punctuality.

12. The duration of each visit should be at least 45 minutes unless otherwise specified by the owners. This includes your traveling time and allows enough time to perform the necessary duties and provide quality playtime for the pets. They will be lonesome and very excited to see you. Plan on supplying lots of affection.

13. Alternate lighting if specified. Most homes have timers on their lamps to go on and off automatically. Double check all doors and confirm the house is secure. Be sure everyone is happy and healthy. Inspect all other rooms daily. There will be occasions when you may find a few hidden surprises where they should not be, if you know what I mean!

14. Make sure the pets eat their meals in your presence. Be certain they relieve themselves regularly and normally. These are two primary occurrences that you must see with your own eyes daily! Make this a significant part of your daily routine. A watery stool or diarrhea is a warning signal. If it continues for more than 24 hours, call the veterinarian.

Always check to be sure the cats use the litter box. A pet's eyes should be bright and responsive. Granted, some pets are a little shy, but do not overlook the chance of a problem. There are home-use veterinarian guide publications that I advise you to purchase from any local book store. They will help to familiarize you with symptoms of illnesses you should be able to detect immediately. The slightest change in a pet's behavior should alert you that something is wrong. Successful treatment can be given if the ailment is diagnosed early enough. Many symptoms are common to more than one illness. Do not attempt a diagnosis on your own. Here are some warning signals:

- Drinking excessive amounts of water

- Frequency in urinating

- Litter box unused

- Urinating in unusual areas of the house

- Abnormal breathing

- Persistent coughing

- Loss of appetite

- Lethargy

- Changes in behavior

15. Before leaving the home, account for all pets. Take the dog out for a last pit stop and say goodnight to all. Lock the door and double check it.

16. On your very last pet visit, the day your clients return home, clean the house. Change the cat litter. Wash all dishes and utensils. Remove the garbage and place a new plastic garbage bag in the can. Leave them a note telling them how well-behaved everyone was and report any health problems or trips to the vet. Chances are, if you did go to the vet, you were in touch with the owners. Relate some of the amusing antics that went on. Never say anything negative about the pet. Tell them how much of a pleasure it was to care for their pets.

Chapter 15

A Day in the Life
of a Professional Petsitter

The best way to expose you to the world of petsitting is to take you through a simulated Murphy's Law Day, chock full of petsittings, including some of the adventures you may experience. Pay close attention to the way I handle problems that arise.

Monday Morning, 6:00 A.M.

The alarm clock rings and up I jump, ready to confront another day of petsitting. Showered and dressed, I make my way into my home office. I converted the spare bedroom into my office. My very first job is to check the petsitting schedule for the day. The weekly schedule is written on a 4' x 4' dry erase board. The names of the customers and the times they are to be tended to are scheduled two weeks in advance. The board is set up to read from Sunday through Sunday. The board is updated on a regular basis and the information is taken directly from the appointment book where I schedule all petsittings as my customers request them.

My first appointment of the day is at 8:00 A.M. They are new customers, the Wileys, with two Lhasa Apsos named Harry and Sally. I plan to be early for the sit because I like to spend extra time with new pets to help them through the transition period. I give them lots of extra attention. The majority of the pets take well to the petsitting experience but others do not. That's why it's a good idea to be a little more concerned with new clients. My next three appointments are scheduled for 9:00 A.M. , 10:00 and 11:00. They are all cat sitting customers. At noon and at 12:45 P.M. I have scheduled two mid-day walks on the east side of town in close proximity to one another.

My next appointment isn't until 3:00 P.M. That gives me time to come back home, have lunch and return telephone calls that may have come in. At 3:00, it's back to the Wileys for the second visit of the day. The Wileys specifically requested three visits each day for their dogs. At 4:00, a house check is scheduled and at 5:00, 6:00 and 7:00, three cat sitting customers are to be cared for. I have noted on the board that the Johnson's cat is to be medicated on the 5:00 visit, due to a respiratory infection. My last appointment of the day is at 8:00 P.M. and it is the last visit for the Wileys. It is a very full day. I make it a habit to write down my schedule on the Daily Schedule Sheet, Form #5. My next step is to check the telephone answering machine to see if anyone has called since I last checked. The answering machine is clear. I put on my digital beeper and I am now ready to start my day. I remove my customer files from the locking file cabinet that only I have access to. I check each file to be sure the keys are secure in their envelopes.

I place the customer files in my locking briefcase and place it into the trunk of my car. On the front seat, I have a clipboard with the Mileage Log Sheet, Form #31 or Form #32, which contains more detailed information. I check the odometer and record the mileage before I start out. When I get to my destination, I record the reading again and so on. Since I need gas before I start work, I head to a gas station on the way to my client and fill up. I save the receipt for income tax purposes and list the amount on the weekly vehicle expense report, form #15.

I arrive at the Wileys at 7:30 A.M. Unlocking the trunk, I open my briefcase and remove the Wiley customer file. I pull the house keys and quickly review some of the specifics of the visit. I check the mail and pick up the newspaper. I give the home a quick, overall examination. All seems fine. As I walk toward the front door, I hear the dogs barking. I unlock the door and open it slowly, place the house keys into my pocket and call out to Harry and Sally. Here they come running! I then hear a strange loud beping sound. Oh no! I forgot to check the file to see if there was a burglar alarm! I quickly reach into my customer file and pull out the Burglar Alarm Information Sheet, #8, to retrieve the code, but too late! The alarm is shrieking! The information sheet includes information to record the steps to follow in the event of the accidental tripping of the alarm. In this particular case, the alarm company will call the Wileys residence within two minutes of receiving the alarm signal. Before they call the police, they will request my name and a secret password previously registered on file by the Wileys. Some companies require a secret number. The phone rings, I answer and relay the information. They are satisfied and the alarm is shut off automatically. Whew! I take a deep breath, compose myself and proceed with the petsit. Where are the dogs? No doubt they are in shock from the whole incident and have probably dug a hole to China by now! How could I have forgotten the alarm? This incident has really taught me a lesson. Always check the customer file thoroughly before entering a home. Know what to expect.

I call out the dog's names. Here they come! They are wagging their tails vigorously and jumping on me. They are so happy to see me, especially without the wailing siren. We become reacquainted with one another and I set out to find and attach their leashes. As I try to hook up Sally's leash, Harry is jumping on me as I grapple with the clip. After a few minutes of struggling, I finally hook Sally and attempt Harry. Now Sally is jumping all over me, pouncing on my back and leaping through the air, landing on my lap! Help!! Finally, Harry is fastened. They pull me out the front door at the speed of sound. They certainly have a lot of energy! I keep a tight grip on both leashes, confident they cannot slip out of my grasp. I lock the door behind me and proceed down the street where the Wileys had instructed me to walk the dogs. At the end of the road is a vacant lot where the dogs must do their business. Never let a dog go on a neighbor's lawn unless you are carrying a pooper scooper. I walk them for a few minutes until I KNOW their business is complete.

We come back home, I unleash the dogs and check the customer file to see if the dogs are to be fed in the morning or the evening. They split one can of food in the morning and have an abundant supply of dry food all day. I also check the water bowl. After they have eaten, I discard the pet food can into the recycling bin and wash the bowls to get them ready for the next day. The dogs are content. I spend time playing with them by throwing a tennis ball down the hallway. After a bit of fun, I make a quick check of all the doors and windows. I attempt to leave, but Harry is following me with a look of disappointment on his face. I assure him that I will be back and give them both a biscuit. I reset the burglar alarm by punching the code into the alarm keypad on the wall. I have 15 seconds to exit. I place the key back into the customer file key envelope and put the file back into the trunk.

Off to my next sit. I check my schedule for the next appointment. The Hogans are next on the agenda. They have three cats. Two are Siamese and one is a red tabby. They are all so beautiful. Same routine as before. I enter with my hands down toward the bottom of the door so the cats do not scurry out the door through my legs. I stack the mail neatly on the dining room table and put the newspaper on the kitchen counter. So far, only Mickey has made an appearance. I search for Minnie and Red, checking every room in the house, looking under the beds and in the closets. I still haven't found them, but I don't panic because there are plenty of hiding places that cats love.

I check under the bathroom cabinets. I check behind the wall unit, and under the couch in the living room. I search the garage. I work my way into the kitchen. I open the cabinets under the sink and who do I find hiding behind the wastebasket?? Minnie and Red! I try to coax them out by talking to them softly, but I do not try to reach in and grab them. They weren't budging. I decided to get on with my chores and started to open their food. The sound of the electric can opener opening their can of food did the trick. They all came running to eat! As they feast, I walk around outside the home to be sure that all the windows and doors are secure. I scoop out and sweep up around the litter box. I perform a general clean up and check the file to see what days to set out the garbage. The sanitation department comes by tomorrow morning so I need to put the trash can by the curb as I am leaving. I will not be back until 9:00 the next morning and by then it will be too late. Once finished, I am off again.

My next visit is to Mrs. Evans' home. She is a widower and lives alone with her 16-year-old cat, Felix. Felix needs extra special attention on every visit because he truly misses his companion when she takes off on business trips. He is an older cat and I need to be cognizant of any changes in his eating habits or his mood, which may indicate illness.

Felix has special dietary food prescribed by the veterinarian. I spoon his food into his dish and wash and refill his water bowl. Felix isn't too interested in his food, which is OK, but I will make a note to check to see that he has eaten his food on my next visit. One definite sign of sickness is lack of appetite. I change the litter and place the refuse in the outside garbage receptacle. Felix is laying on his favorite chair gazing out the window watching the birds. I sit by him and spend time petting and talking to him. He purrs loudly. Mrs. Evans has stipulated that under no circumstances am I to give Felix any treats because he does not digest food well. I re-check the file to see if there are any additional instructions. I kiss Felix goodbye and prepare to go to my next client.

My next petsit is about ten miles from my last visit. The quickest route to take is the Interstate Highway. Cruising along at 55 m.p.h., my car begins to stall and steam is billowing out from under the hood. My car has overheated!! I coast to the side of the highway, lock my car and walk to the nearest pay phone. I telephone AAA Auto Club and make arrangements for my car and then I telephone my sister, who is my backup petsitter. I have trained her to take over for me in emergency situations. She knows the clients and pets and will meet me to pick up the customer files and perform the petsit while my car is repaired.

By 2 P.M. I am back in the driver's seat. As I prepare to head home my beeper goes off. It is my sister. I return the call. She has finished the last mid-day walk and was concerned about the rest of the day. I assured her my car is running and we make arrangements to meet back at the house to return the customer files.

Back at the Wileys at 3:00. I check the mail. This time, I disengage the burglar alarm upon entry. I stack the letters in an orderly fashion. I walk the dogs and play tug-o-war with an old sock the dogs have brought to me. I recheck the entire home and turn on the living room and bedroom light per the Wiley's instructions. I give the dogs a treat, pat them on the head and switch on the outside light because I will be back again this evening when it is dark. I reset the alarm, lock and double check the door and place the key back into the envelope and return it to the trunk of my car.

Two house checkups are next on the itinerary. Upon arrival, I remove the Housewatching/ Housesitting Inspection and Condition report from the file, Form #18, attach it to the clipboard and record information as I inspect the interior and exterior of the property. I note the condition of the house and if there are any repairs or problems to tend to. These completed forms must be sent to the owners of the homes on a weekly basis. Communication with the homeowners is paramount. The check up is complete. I recheck the lighting and lock the door as I depart.

It is 4:30 P.M. I drive to the Johnsons to care for Jesse. He is a six-month-old Himalayan plagued for two weeks by a respiratory infection that he just cannot shake. I reread the instructions from Form #15, Medication Instruction Sheet, and administer the two cc's of amoxicillin called for on the sheet. I bring in the mail and newspapers and remove the pizza advertisement hanging from the doorknob. I enter the home and call to Jesse. He usually meets me at the door. I find him crouched over the water dish and he seems extremely lethargic. I pick him up and notice that he has an excessive amount of mucous flowing from his nostrils. His eyes are extremely watery. He is doesn't respond to my voice. I immediately go into the file, pull out Form #16, Veterinarian Medical Release form, and call Jesse's veterinarian. The answering service answers as Jesse's regular vet is out of town. They refer me to a clinic about five miles from the client's home. I immediately call the owners at the out-of-town telephone number on Form #10, General Information Sheet, to inform them of the situation. I leave a message to call me at their earliest convenience. I place Jesse in the plastic cat carrier left by the owners and rush him to the clinic. They take us without delay and give Jesse a complete medical checkup. He has a temperature and tell me they must keep him overnight. I agree and give them my telehone number and ask that they please call me and keep be abreast of the situation. The clinic requires payment for the initial visit. I write them a company check, which I carry for just such emergencies. I will be reimbursed by the owner and I will be sure to include the extra charges on the invoice. I visit Jesse in his little cage back in the infirmary and reassure him that he will be fine.

I head to my next two cat sitting appointments. I call my answering machine to retrieve any phone calls that may have come in. I return the calls and write down all appointments in my book. I try again to reach Jesse's owners, but still no answer. I finish caring for my cat customers and head out on the road again.

It is now 7:30 P.M. and I head back to the Wileys for their last walk of the day. However, as I pull up into the driveway, I instantly notice that something is wrong. I know I had left two lights on inside the home and I also switched on the outside light for security purposes on my last visit. No lights are illuminated whatsoever. As I proceed closer to the house, I notice that the garage window is broken. Without hesitation, I drive away to the nearest phone booth and telephone the police. I do not enter the home under any circumstances. I tell them that I am the petsitter and that the owners are out of town and there may be a possible break in. They are immediately dispatched to the residence. I arrive shortly after the police have investigated the home. Its seems as though there was an attempted forced entry into the home and the burglar alarm was somehow disconnected. The electricity was also shut off. Luckily, the burglars never made it into the home. I immediately rushed in to make sure Harry and Sally were all right. They were fine and were already making new friends with the police officers. The power was switched back on and the alarm was reengaged. I requested a police report and called the Wileys to inform them of what had transpired. I also boarded up the garage window with a piece of plywood. Finally, I walked the dogs and upon returning, placed a call to the veterinary clinic to check up on Jesse's condition. The vet reported that all was satisfactory and that there was a slight improvement in Jesse's condition. In fact, they thought I would be able to pick him up in the morning. I then called Jesse's owners and they were pleased that I had acted so responsibly and without hesitation. I gave Harry and Sally their last treat of the day, reset the alarm and headed out the door.

As I drive away, I am satisfied with the outcome of the day. I am pleased that I was competent enough to handle all the problems that arose. I was able to keep my cool by following instructions and using common sense to deal with the situations that occurred. I had trained and educated myself thoroughly on how to overcome obstacles that may occur during the course of a regular petsitting day.

Once home, I update my schedule for the next day and look forward to another day of petsitting, although not a repeat of this day, I hope! But I wouldn't have traded it for any other. The rewards are well worth the effort.

Chapter 16

Business Information Sources

The following business information sources are a welcome helping hand to the new business owner. Please retain the subsequent list and call for assistance when necessary.

1. **American Business Woman's Association**
    9100 Ward Parkway
    Kansas City, Mo 64114-0728
    Phone: (816)361-6621

2. **Charities Information Bureau**
    19 Union Square West
    New York, New York 10003
    Phone: (212)929-6300

3. **Copyright Office**
    Library of Congress
    101 Independence Avenue, SE
    Washington, DC 20559
    Phone: (202)287-5000
    Forms Hotline: (202)287-9100

4. If you cannot find the Small Business Administration in your local telephone book under U.S. Government, write or call:

    Small Business Administration
    1441 L Street, NW
    Washington, DC 20416
    Phone: (202)653-6365
    *Request a copy of *Small Business Tax Workshop,* **IRS Publication #1057**

5. **International Franchise Association**
    1350 New York Avenue, NW
    Washington, DC 20005
    Phone: (202)628-8000

6. **Office of Information and Public Affairs**
    U.S. Department of Labor
    200 Constitution Avenue, NW
    Washington, DC 20210
    Phone: (202)523-7316

7. **United States Postal Service**
    National 5 Digit Zip and Post Office Directory
    Address Information Center
    Memphis, TN 38188-9980

8. **United States Department of Labor**
    200 Constitution Avenue, NW
    Washington, DC 20210
    Phone: (202)523-7316

9. **SCORE (Service Corps of Retired Executives)**

    An Organization sponsored by the Small Business Administration. These men and women **volunteer** their services to small business owners who need help.

    SCORE
    The Small Business Administration
    1441 L. Street NW
    Washington, DC 20416
    Phone: (202)653-6365 Consult your local phone directory for a SCORE office near you.

10. **Wage and Salary Information**
    The Bureau of Labor Statistics
    Superintendent of Documents
    Washington, DC 20403

11. **Small Business Administration Free Publications**
    Management Assistance Publications
    1441 L. Street
    Washington, DC 20416

12. **Small Business Publications for Sale**
    Superintendents of Documents
    Washington, DC 20402

    Ask for subject bibliographies.

13. **Internal Revenue Service**
Washington, DC 20224

14. **International Franchise Association**
1350 New York Avenue, NW
Washington, DC 20005
(202)628-8000

15. **National Small Business United**
1155 15th Street, NW
Washington, DC 20005
(202)293-8830

Petsitting's popularity has prompted the formation of several membership organizations catering specifically to petsitters throughout the country. They provide essential information pertaining to the petsitting industry. These associations also function as a referral service for their members. They circulate a newsletter containing up-to-date information for petstters everywhere. Some of these organizations include:

1. **Pet Sitters Association of Southern California**
P.O. Box 5432
Whittier, California 90607-5432

2. **National Association of Pet Sitters**
632 Holly Avenue
Winston-Salem, North Carolina 27101

3. **American Pet Sitting Club**
61 S. Division Street
New Rochelle, New York 10805

Chapter 17

Hiring The Helper

The most valuable resources of any business are those people who represent it. There are many honorable and sincere animal lovers willing and eager to join your new enterprise. There are those you will have good feelings about and those you will have reservations about. If you intend to run a one-person operation, it is only common sense that you should have a back up. What if you become ill and are unable to carry out your scheduled appointments, who will take over for you? Your customers will expect an answer. Prepare yourself accordingly. Train a family member or friend as an emergency replacement or hire a helper. A properly trained petsitter is a more reliable option.

Petsitting is an exclusive occupation. Keep in mind that whoever you choose to work with must be of impeccable character. They must unequivocally love pets! All prospective applicants must be bondable! Instruct all candidates to fill out an application, plus an addendum to the application (Forms #37 and #38).

Conduct a personal interview with the applicant. Insist they furnish you with a resume. Uncover as much as you can about the person's character. Do they have a pleasant personality? What experience do they have with pets? Do they have pets of their own? Discuss the job description. Describe in detail the tasks they will perform. Would they like this type of work?

Telephone all former employers and question why this person no longer works there. Would they rehire them? Investigate references thoroughly. References for the potential employee or independent contractor cannot be relatives or friends. Letters of recommendation are a plus.

Any doubts or questions about the integrity of the prospective worker may spell trouble for the unsuspecting business owner. You will be entrusting the person you hire with confidential information pertaining to your clients. They will have the keys to their homes and the responsibility of their pets' lives. You must be 100 percent convinced of their honesty, decency, and respectability before hiring them.

I required all prospective employees to obtain a Police Identification Card from the local police department in the city where they live. Their fingerprints and photograph are on file should anything happen. My most dependable and trustworthy workers were my friends and relatives. I felt more at ease working with those I knew on a personal level. You can never be too careful.

Before placing an ad for help in your local newspaper, telephone nearby veterinarians. They may know of some real animal lovers. Perhaps some of their receptionists or technicians might be looking for part-time work. It helps if the person you are hiring is recommended by someone you know. Put up flyers at colleges, libraries, women's organizations, or your local humane society. These are excellent sources for helpers. If you place an ad in the classifieds, do so in publications located in the targeted territories requiring help.

Do not over hire. First, try a weekend helper to lessen the load a little. Grow into hiring as you gain more customers. Petsitting is a highly personalized service and keeping tabs on too many workers can become quite burdensome. I suggest you hire two helpers and no more. Hire more as you expand your customer base. You must be extremely organized to run an operation that employs three or more workers. However, it can be accomplished. By my third year in business, I employed ten workers. I equipped each worker with a digital pager in order to reach them throughout the day.

Conduct personal checkups of your employee's work. There is another way to insure proper work performance. Provide each worker with a Customer Comment Sheet, Form #20, to leave with the customer on the final sitting day. Ask your customers to fill this out and send it aong with their payment. The efficiency rating spans from poor to excellent. I provided additional space for customer comments.

Holidays are your busiest and most lucrative time periods. Arrange the petsitting work schedule in accordance with the sitter's preference. Everyone should spend quality time with their families during the holidays. Christmas, Thanksgiving, Easter, the Fourth of July, and Memorial Day tend to be favorites.

The Personnel File

You must create a personnel file on every worker you hire. The following forms must be filled out and signed by you and your helper before they can begin to work for you:

Form #37 - Application For Employment

Form #38 - Addendum To Employment Application

Form #9 - Bonding Company Information Notice

Form #43 - Employee/Contractor Confidentiality Agreement

Form #39 - Consent to Release of Employment Information

Form #44 or #41- Independent Contractor Agreement

Form #45 - Night Shift Agreement (if applicable)

Form #42 - Employee/Contractor Non-Compete Agreement

Form #40 - Employment Contract (if applicable)

IRS Form - W-4 Form (if applicable)

Proof of citizenship or resident alien status.

Properly Supplying The Pet Sitter

The following forms must be supplied to your helpers for them to perform their duties thoroughly:

Form #20 - Customer Comment Sheet

Form #32 - Weekly Motor Vehicle Expense Report

Form #31- Mileage Log Sheet

Form #47 - Employee/Contractor Weekly Time Sheet and Mileage Report

Furnish the following items for your petsitter:

1. Leash

2. Flashlight and extra batteries

3. Appointment book

4. Pooper scooper

5. Plastic garbage bags

6. Company letterhead and pen (for last visit notes)

7. Local map

8. Schedule of appointments

9. Flyers, brochures and business cards (to promote the business)

10. Veterinary first aid kit and emergency manual

11. Umbrella and rain gear

12. Can of mace

13. Digital beeper

Pay your workers as well as your budget will allow. Minimum wage will not suffice. Give people an incentive to work hard and feel proud of their accomplishments. I paid $5 per hour and 15 cents per mile for gas mileage to start. The U.S. government approved mileage reimbursement is 28 cents per mile. Set up your own payment plan or follow government standards. You and your helper can agree on a fair evaluation. Train your helpers thoroughly. Familiarize everyone with all forms and agreements. I personally trained all workers and guided them through the correct procedures. Take them with you on petsitting visits. Explain step-by-step the tasks you expect them to perform. Furnish them with a checklist of duties. This reassures you the jobs were done thoroughly and per your instructions. Set them off on their own when you are 100% convinced they are ready. Usually two weeks of training is necessary. After a 30-day probationary period, I raised their wages to $6 per hour. Of course, any tips or gifts from customers were theirs to keep.

All business organizations are capable of protecting trade secrets, sales territories and customer information. Business owners often find it is helpful to place the terms of their employment into a binding Employment Contract. You will find an Employment Contract and a Non-Compete Agreement also included (see Forms #40 and #42). These agreements outline company policies and hold anyone who works in your company liable if they chose to leave and start their own petsitting service. They could steal your customers away if you are not protected. You must safeguard yourself in every way possible.

Always praise your helpers for a job well done. Express your appreciation for their conscientious care. Show concern for their problems. Let them know they can come to you with any questions they have. Continually offer your help and support to them.

Chapter 18

Paying Your Helper

Traditionally, the employer hires the employee and assumes the responsibility of retaining federal withholding taxes and Social Security taxes. The employer must carry workers compensation insurance, pay payroll, Social Security taxes and unemployment compensation taxes. If you have no experience with these procedures, your accountant or bookkeeper can explain it to you. If you should decide to hire your employees this way, your kit contains a legally prepared Employment Contract, Form #40.

Under the law, every individual who performs services subject to the will and control of an employer is an employee. Every individual told what to do and how it shall be done is an employee.

Each employee must fill out a W-4 Form his or her first day of work. This form is available through the IRS. It documents the employee's Social Security number and how many dependents he or she will claim. You will use this information to determine the amount of the withholding tax deduction.

Withholding taxes are those funds withheld from your employee's gross wages in accordance with IRS guidelines. The IRS publication, Circular E, contains the applicable tax tables and instructions for these withholding methods. Any funds withheld are deposited into a federal tax depository customarily located at your local bank. You are accountable for depositing payroll taxes. The IRS will send you a withholding tax payment booklet and rules for depositing once you have obtained your federal tax identification number.

Another tax that is deducted from your employee's gross wages is the Social Security tax, or FICA, the Federal Insurance Contribution Act.

Social Security taxes become levied on both the employer and the employee. In essence, the employer pays half of the employee's Social Security tax. You will need to obtain the current Social Security tax rate to calculate the precise deductions from the Social Security Administration.

You are also responsible for unemployment compensation taxes. This tax provides payments to workers who have lost their jobs. A tax rate assigned to you along with instructions on how and where to file are on the form the state will mail to you.

I did not hire my helpers in this manner. Depending on how you intend to operate your business, it is your decision on how you hire and pay your workers.

The character of the petsitting business is not always a set, hourly arrangement where your worker must report to work every day. There may be no daily fixed schedule. Therefore, an alternative method of engaging help is the implementation of independent contractor or subcontractor status. It is a more simplified method of payment and a definite decrease in paperwork.

Independent contractors work their own schedules. They are self-employed individuals. They have the choice to perform a petsitting job or to turn the job down. Calculate their paychecks by each job or at an hourly rate of pay. They are solely responsible for their own withholding taxes, Social Security taxes, worker's compensation insurance and health insurance. They must *sign* an independent contractor's acknowledgement with you. See Forms #44 and #41. They will also need to fill out the following Forms: #43, #39, #32, #31, #45 and #47.

A 1099 Miscellaneous Income form is a yearly statement of wages. By law you must issue one to each independent contractor who earns over $600 in one year. The independent contractor is responsible for filing their personal income taxes. The IRS has conditional guidelines that you must follow in order to hire under the independent subcontractor's status. Be diligent in your decision to hire this way, because the IRS is very strict about adhering to these guidelines.

Chapter 19

Computerize If You Can

Computers are everywhere!! They are learning tools for our children in school and used in businesses all over the world. If you have a personal computer, of course it is a plus. If you do not, it is not essential. But computers can definitely make our lives and our businesses easier to manage.

As my business grew, so did the need for a computer. I bought a used IBM compatible for a very small investment. I used a word processing program, which saved me a lot of time writing letters and preparing forms for the Information Packages. By educating myself with the program's capabilities, I eventually designed my own forms and agreements. I stored them on disks for future use. This saved greatly on printing costs. You can do the same.

There are countless prepackaged, ready-to-use computer programs that can do everything from handling your financial affairs to playing video games. I suggest a word processing program to help you design business forms and construct a client data base that will enable you to print out address labels for bulk mailouts. Your accountant may be able to suggest appropriate software for your business.

You can perform your bookkeeping functions and invoice your clients from an accounting program suitable for you. I also suggest you consider a spreadsheet program called Lotus 1-2-3. This spreadsheet program is a super calculator with columns and rows where you enter numbers and store them in the memory of the computer. You can add and subtract figures with the stroke of a key. Vocational/technical schools and community colleges offer computer classes. They teach classes from basic computer training to advanced instruction.

By computerizing, you open the door to boundless sources of modernized business strengths! By all means, computerize and devise your own mode of operation. The average home office today has a personal computer, printer, answering machine and telephone. Today a home-operated business needs to use as much of the latest technology as possible. Classified ads are a good way to find buys on used computers and software. Another avenue would be to call on computer stores with trade-ins. Complete set-ups for around $500 can be found. Be sure to get a computer with a reputation for reliability. Do not purchase a Brand X you have never heard of before, even if the price is right.

Selecting a printer is also a very important consideration because it will depict your professional image to your customers and to others affiliated with your business. A dot matrix printer is the least expensive and can produce letter quality printing for all of your business correspondence.

Chapter 20

Choosing a Commercial Printer

Plan to visit three or four printing establishments. Gather quotes and lettering ideas for your brochures, stationery, billheads, checks, etc. Your stationery and business cards give customers that very first impression of your company. Remember, you can never get a second chance to make a good first impression! It is so important to choose colors and designs carefully. Be sure to list the services of the petsitter on your business card. It acts as an instant brochure. Unless you prefer to use colored paper, it is less expensive to use white paper with black lettering on letterheads, envelopes, business cards and brochures. Also, the larger the order the less expensive the unit costs become.

Printers perform countless functions for the new business owner. They provide graphic design and layout, computerized typesetting, color printing, copying, binding, desktop publishing, collating, mailing list management, logo creation, foil stamping, laminating, lithography, digital typography, die cutting, fax communications, and direct mail services.

They create letterheads, envelopes, announcements, booklets, brochures, business cards, flyers, carbonless business forms, rubber stamps, newsletters, mailers, computer forms, labels, catalogs, manuals, resumes, and invitations.

The cost of paper and number of ink colors you choose are surely a pricing factor. Rates climb if you require both sides of the paperwork printed. Be sure printing quotes include folding, cutting, stamping, or embossing.

An expert printer helps boost your professional look! Remember also, a printer with the lowest price quote may not be the finest. Quality is what you are looking for at reasonable rates.

Chapter 21

Housesitting/Housewatching Exclusively

Dependable housesitting/housewatching is a service you can provide away from the pet-sitting aspect of your company. Although it is an extension of your petsitting services, there are many petless homeowners who need their homes, condominiums, apartments and townhomes looked after while they are away. There are those housesitters who may opt to stay within the home and sleep in the home for a specified period of time. If your lifestyle allows you this freedom, then by all means, pursue this type of arrangement.

The alternative to staying over is to provide periodic checkups inside and outside of the home. Check once per month, twice per month and so on. Generally, most homeowners want a weekly checkup if they are to be gone for one month or more in order to be sure that all is well. Those who take vacations need their homes checked daily to bring in the mail and newspapers, alternate the lighting, and do a quick check in and around the home.

Housewatching/housesitting exclusively is petsitting minus the pet. Follow the same instructions as mentioned in Chapter 12, "The Initial Interview." The owners will provide you with a list of the contractors who take care of the lawn, pool, pest control, cleaning personnel, etc., and their phone numbers so you may reach them if a problem arises. Ask the owners exactly what they need you to do. Fill out Form #17.

It can be very lucrative for an aggressive businessperson to explore this added service. Here is a checklist of the services you will provide. You will be the eyes and ears of the absentee owner.

1. Upon your arrival to the home, do a visual perusal of the property and walk the perimeter to make sure all doors and windows have remained locked and secure. Take in any mail or newspapers or doorknob flyers from the premises.

2. Enter the home, noting the lights which are to be left on. Make sure they are still on. If the lights are on timers, check the timers to be sure they are working.

3. Double check all doors and windows including sliding glass doors and be certain all locks are secure. If watching a home, check that the garage door is locked.

4. Flush all toilets.

5. Run tap water from all faucets.

6. Check plumbing for leaks.

7. Check A/C, thermostat and humidistat.

8. Check circuit breakers and light bulbs.

9. Check closets.

10. Check ceilings and walls.

11. Water the plants.

12. Check for insects and rodents.

13. Make sure the security system is working.

14. Make sure the pool is being tended to.

15. Make sure the lawn maintenance is being done.

16. Turn on the irrigation system to be sure no sprinkler heads have been broken, therefore spewing excessive amounts of water from the pipes.

17. Start the car if called for.

18. Open and close vertical blinds if necessary.

19. Upon the return of the owner, you must open up the house, air it out and do some light dusting for a pleasant welcome home.

The homeowner will stipulate the instructions to be followed. A brief, written condition report, dated, and a copy sent to the owner will follow every inspection (Form #18). Retain a copy for your records. You will also need to use Forms #6, #7, and #13. Leave the invoice in the home on the counter or table with a "welcome home" note and any comments you need to make. I suggest that you charge a homeowner $50 per month and up for housesitting, making four house checkups per month.

Appendix One

Petsitting and Housewatching Business Forms and Contracts

Business Forms

The following list of business forms corresponds numerically with the subsequent business forms herewith. These are sample forms you may photocopy for your own use or employ these ideas to create your own forms. After you have photocopies, type your business name, address and telephone number in the spaces provided.

1. **Information Letter:** Accompanies information package that is sent to inquiring customer.

2. **Sample Reference Form**

3. **Customer Call-In Report and Reservation Time Sheet**: Information filled out on every individual caller.

4. **Follow-Up Letter to Information Package:** Sent when no response is heard after sending an information package to a caller.

5. **Daily Schedule Sheet**

6. **General Release Form:** Releases you from liability and lists additional persons who will access the home during the period you will be petsitting.

7. **General Release Form and Disclaimer of Liability:** Releases you from any claim of liability.

8. **Natural Disaster Instruction Sheet:** Used in those areas prone to hurricanes, tornadoes, earthquakes, flooding, etc.

9. **Bonding Company Information Notice:** Lists names of those to be covered under the dishonesty bond.

10. **General Information Sheet:** To be filled out at the initial interview with customer and placed in the customer file.

11. **Release for Key on File**: Grants you permission to retain house key on file.

12. **Postal Release**: Grants permission to sign for customer's mail being held at the post office.

13. **Burglar Alarm Information Sheet**: Lists alarm company and code.

14. **Pet Data and Information Sheet**: To be filled out at the initial interview and placed in the customer file.

15. **Medication Instruction Sheet**: To be used when medication must be administered.

16. **Veterinarian Medical Emergency Release Form**: Grants you permission to take a customer's pet to a veterinarian or emergency clinic in case of illness or accident.

17. **Housewatching Checklist**: Used when caring for a home only.

18. **Housewatching/Housesitting Inspection and Condition Report**

19. **Interior of Property**

20. **Customer Comment Sheet**: Customer rates the quality of the service.

21. **Sample Newspaper Article/Press Release**

22. **Sample Press Release**

23. **Sample Thank You Letter to Publications**

24. **Sample Business Announcement to Veterinarians**

25. **Holiday Reminder Notices**

26. **Complimentary Anniversary Gift Certificate**

27. **Sample Price Increase Letter**

28. **Sample Brochure**

29. **Accounts Receivable Log**: Records all unpaid invoices.

30. **Sample Invoice**: Lists dates of petsitting and total amount charged to a customer.

31. **Mileage Log Sheet**: Records daily mileage and weekly total.

32. **Weekly Motor Vehicle Expense Report**: Lists amounts spent for gasoline, oil, tolls, etc.

33. **Request for Payment Letter**

34. **Late Payment Reminder**

35. **Notice of Dishonored Check**: Notifies customer of dishonored check.

36. **Employment Inquiry Response Letter**: Respond to employee inquiries.

37. **Application for Employment**

38. **Addendum to Employment Application**: Provides additional information on the employee/contractor.

39. **Consent to Release of Employment Information**: Used to obtain additional information on prospective workers.

40. **Employment Contract**

41. **Independent Contractor Acknowledgment**

42. **Employee Non-Compete Agreement**: Employee/contractor agrees not to initiate his/her own petsitting service and other covenants.

43. **Confidentiality Agreement**: Employee/Contractor agree not to divulge any information pertaining to the business and clientele.

44. **Independent Contractor Agreement**

45. **Independent Contractor Pay Sheet**

46. **Night Shift Agreement**: Emloyee/Contractor agreement to work at night.

47. **Employee/Contractor Weekly Time Sheet and Mileage Report**: Weekly report from your employee reporting hours worked and mileage used on each job.

48. **Resignation Letter**: Signed by employee when resigning from employment with you.

#1 / Information Letter

Date
Name
Address

Thank you for your interest in _____. We are proud of our services and of our reputation as well. Please find enclosed a brochure and references for you to review. We encourage you to call all of the enclosed references. Please look over the literature and feel free to give us a call to set up an appointment to meet with us. Thank you very much.

Sincerely,

_____

#2 / Sample Reference Form

PET SITTING SERVICES, INC.
REFERENCES

Customer City
Customer Name
Customer Phone Number

_____
110-8062

_____
110-8888

_____
110-4966

_____
110-6749

_____
110-2345

Boynton Beach

_____
110-1463

_____
110-1259

_____
711-2091

Deerfield Beach

_____
110-5448

_____
116-8941

#2, continued

Veterinarians And Pet Shops

_____ Animal Clinic
Pompano Beach
Dr. _____ , DVM
Dr. _____ , DVM

_____

_____ Animal Clinic
Boca Raton
Dr. _____ , DVM

_____

_____ Animal Hospital
Delray Beach
Dr. _____ , DVM
Dr. _____ , DVM

_____

Pet Paraphernalia, Inc.
Fort Lauderdale

_____

_____

Pet Haven

_____

_____

The Better Business Bureau of Palm Beach County

_____

_____

#3 / Customer Call-In Report and Reservation Time Sheet

Customer name   Date of call
_____

Customer telephone number
_____

Address
_____

City/St/Zip
_____

New Customer   Yes   No
_____

How did they hear about us?
_____

Newspaper Issue date
_____

Other
_____

# of pets
_____

Types of pets: (cats, dogs, birds?)
_____

Medical problems?
_____

Send information package?   Yes   No
_____

Prices quoted
_____

Initial interview   Date sheduled
_____

Key status: On file   Pick up   Mailed
_____

Pick up date and time
_____

Departure and Return Information
_____

Departure date and time
_____

First visit/date and time
_____

Last visit/date and time
_____

Return date and time
_____

#3, continued

Out-Of-Town Emergency Phone Number

_____

_____

_____

Additional information and instructions

_____

_____

_____

_____

_____

Has the above information been posted to appointment book?

_____

File pulled?

_____

Please be sure all information is verified with the customer.

#4 / Follow-Up Letter to Information Package

Date

Name
Address
City/St/Zip

Dear _____

Hello again! We haven't heard from you since we sent out the information you requested. We thought we would take this time to remind you that we are the most reliable and loving alternative to placing your pet in a kennel while you are away. We urge you to call now to set up an interview to meet with us! Please call (___) _____-_____

Thank you!

Sincerely,

_____

#5 / Daily Schedule Sheet

Date

Time	Client Name and Address	Comments
5:00 A.M.		
5:30 A.M.		
6:00 A.M.		
6:30 A.M.		
7:00 A.M.		
7:30 A.M.		
8:00 A.M.		
8:30 A.M.		
9:00 A.M.		
9:30 A.M.		
10:00 A.M.		
10:30 A.M.		
11:00 A.M.		
11:30 A.M.		
12:00 NOON		
12:30 P.M.		
1:00 P.M.		
1:30 P.M.		
2:00 P.M.		
2:30 P.M.		
3:00 P.M.		
3:30 P.M.		
4:00 P.M.		
4:30 P.M.		
5:00 P.M.		
5:30 P.M.		
6:00 P.M.		
6:30 P.M.		
7:00 P.M.		
7:30 P.M.		
8:00 P.M.		
8:30 P.M.		
9:00 P.M.		

#6 / General Release Form

For consideration, the undersigned hereby releases, discharges, acquits and forgives _____ from any and all claims, actions, suits, demands, agreements, liabilities and proceedings both at law and in equity arising during the following contracted dates whereas _____ has agreed to care for the pet(s) and/or home of the undersigned. It is understood that the following individuals have permission and may access said property at the same time as _____

Dates: Beginning _____ Ending _____

The following individuals possess a key to my home and have permission to access my home at the same time period I have contracted _____ to care for my pet(s) and/or home:

1. _____ Phone # _____
2. _____ Phone # _____
3. _____ Phone # _____

Property address:

This release shall be binding upon and ensure to the benefits of the parties, their successors, assigns, and personal representatives.

Signed: _____ Date: _____
           Pet Owner

Signed: _____ Date: _____
           Petsitter

#7 / General Release Form And Disclaimer Of Liability

I (we), the undersigned, do hereby grant _____ and its authorized representatives to enter my (our) home located at:

_____

_____

for the time period specified on the accompanying invoice, for the purpose of caring for my (our) pet(s) and/or home while we are away. I (we) will not hold _____ or its authorized representatives liable in any way for anything not due to their negligence.

I will not hold _____ or its authorized representatives liable for any acts of God over which I(we) have no control such as flooding, hurricanes, tornadoes, fire or any other natural disasters including forced entry of our home or for the death of the pets named to be cared for, due to natural causes or an act of God.

I understand and agree to pay the rate of $ _____ per visit to _____. I further understand this rate may increase and I will be informed accordingly of any changes.

Pets' names:

1. _____   2. _____

3. _____   4. _____

5. _____   6. _____

Signed _____ Dated_____
　　　　　　Pet Owner

Signed _____ Dated _____
　　　　　　Owner/President

#8/ Natural Disaster Instruction Sheet

The following information is to be carried out expediently in the event of any weather emergency that may put the lives of the animals in the care of _____ in jeopardy.

In the event that any warnings are issued to the areas in which we are caring for the pets and home of:

_____
Customer name

_____
Address

_____
City/St/Zip

The following instructions are to be carried out:

1. Prepare my home for possible high winds and heavy rains by:

☐ Placing hurricane shutters   ☐ Taping windows

☐ Removing all patio/porch/outdoor furniture

☐ Removing all plants   ☐ Removing all objects capable of being blown over

2. Pets to be kept within the confines of which rooms?

Have arrangements been previously made to board the pets at a boarding facility? ☐ Yes ☐ No
Name and address of boarding facility:

In the case of an imminent natural disaster, food and water will be left in large amounts for the pets and all necessary preparations for their safety and well-being will be carried out.

Additional instructions:

_____

_____

_____

_____

#9 / Bonding Company Information Notice

_____
Customer name
_____
Address
_____
City/St/Zip

Bonding Company:

Please include the following persons to be covered under my bond:

_____
1.
_____
Address
_____
City/St/Zip

_____
2.
_____
Address
_____
City/St/Zip

_____
3.
_____
Address
_____
City/St/Zip

Please send me an updated list of the persons listed under my bond including the above persons. Thank you.

Sincerely,

Signed _____ Dated_____

#10 / General Information Sheet

Name

Address

City/St/Zip

Home phone   Work phone

Out-of-town emergency phone

Home care information:

☐ Windows closed? ☐ Fans? ☐ A/C set? Temp:

☐ Alternate lighting? ☐ Timers? ☐ Which lights: Times on and off:

☐ Open and close curtains? ☐ Blinds ☐ Mail collection? ☐ Newspaper pickup?

☐ Start car?

☐ UPS packages? ☐ Federal Express?

☐ Plant care? Plant locations

Watering instructions

Garbage days?   Receptacle placement?

☐ Dumpster? Location

Location of litter box, litter and scooper

Where to put scoopings

Pooper scooper regulations

Instructions

Location of cleaning supplies

☐ Garbage bags ☐ Broom ☐ Vacuum

Neighbors/police aware of absence?

Neighbor's name and phone number:

Do they have an extra key?   ☐ Yes   ☐ No

#10, continued

Anyone else authorized to enter home in addition to us?

If telephone rings, should we answer?   ☐ Yes   ☐ No
(We never say the owners are out of town.)
Retrieve answering machine messages and reset machine?   ☐ Yes   ☐ No

---

Who to contact if A/C or major appliance fails?

Which door will we be entering and leaving by?
Keys received? For which doors

Additional information

#11 / Release for Key on File

I (we), the undersigned, do hereby authorize _____ to retain in their possession the key(s) to my (our) home on file in a locked filing cabinet or safe, to access my (our) home to care for my (our) pets or home at my (our) specific request.

Signed _____ Dated _____
　　　　　　Pet Owner

Signed _____ Dated _____
　　　　　　Owner/President

#12 / Postal Release

Please permit:

_____

_____

_____

of _____ to collect all of my mail requiring a signature release during the following dates:

_____ thru _____

Signed _____ Dated _____
                 Customer

Signed _____ Dated _____
               Owner/President

#13 / Burglar Alarm Information Sheet

Type of Alarm: ☐ Key ☐ Code

Code Number:

Alarm connected to Security/Police? ☐ Yes ☐ No

Reset Button? ☐ Yes ☐ No

In case of accidental tripping of alarm, the following instructions are to be followed:

Code Word:

Additional Information:

The above information will be used only by _____ with the strict understanding that this information is confidential and only to be used during the specified period of time that the owner designates.

Signed _____ Dated _____
　　　　　　　　Customer

Signed _____ Dated _____
　　　　　　Owner/President

#14 / Pet Data And Information Sheet

Customer name   Customer #
_____

Pets to be cared for: name of pet, type of pet, age, description

1. _____
2. _____
3. _____
4. _____
5. _____

Pet History:
_____

Medical problems: ☐ Yes ☐ No

Past: Present:
_____

If yes, pet names and problems:

_____

_____

_____

_____

Currently being treated?   Medication?

(If so, please use medication administration form.)
_____

Heartworm medication: Days
_____

Amounts
_____

Feeding Instructions:
_____

Cats: type of food and amounts:

Feeding times:

☐ Treats ☐ Vitamins ☐ Catnip
_____

#14, continued

Dogs: type of food and amounts:

Feeding times:

☐ Treats   ☐ Vitamins

Walking areas:

Birds, fish, hamsters, ferrets:

Feeding instructions

Aquarium maintenance instructions

Additional Information:

_____

_____

_____

_____

_____

_____

_____

_____

_____

_____

_____

_____

_____

_____

#15 / Medication Instruction Sheet

Customer name   **Customer #**

Pet(s) to be medicated:

1.   Medical problem

Type of medication

Amounts and # times per day

Medication to end

2.   Medical problem

Type of medication

Amounts and # times per day

Medication to end

3.   Medical problem

Type of medication

Amounts and # times per day

Medication to end

#16 / Veterinarian Medical Emergency Release Form

I,_____, do hereby give _____ full permission and authorization to take my pet and/or pets to my designated veterinarian or pet emergency clinic in the case of sickness or medical emergency. My veterinarian or emergency clinic veterinarian may administer the proper medical attention necessary.

_____
My veterinarian is
_____
Name of clinic
_____
Address
_____
City/St/Zip
_____
Office phone number
_____
Emergency phone number

Signed _____ Dated _____
         Customer

Signed _____ Dated _____
         Owner/President

#17/ Housewatching Checklist

Name

Address

City   Phone

Second home information:

Address

City   State

Phone

Date of departure

Date of return

☐ Weekly checkups   ☐ Biweekly checkups

Day(s) of checkups

Alarm information:

☐ Windows closed   ☐ A/C set   ☐ Mail forwarded   ☐ Newspapers forwarded
☐ Automatic sprinklers

Pool service   Phone

Lawn service   Phone

In case of emergency

Additional Information:

#18 / Housewatching/Housesitting Inspection and Condition Report

Date _____

Property owner's name _____

Property address _____

City/State/Zip _____

Type of property _____

Report submitted by _____

_____

Exterior of Property

Checklist	Condition of Property	Suggestions
1. ☐ Lawn		
2. ☐ Flowers		
3. ☐ Trees		
4. ☐ Shrubs		
5. ☐ Walkways		
6. ☐ Roof		
7. ☐ Windows		
8. ☐ Fence		
9. ☐ Screens		
10. ☐ Driveway		
11. ☐ Pool		
12. ☐ Cleanliness		

Additional comments:

Signed _____ Dated _____

#19 / Interior of Property

Checklist	Condition of Property	Suggestions
1. ☐ Carpeting		
2. ☐ Doors		
3. ☐ Walls		
4. ☐ Baseboards		
5. ☐ Floors		
6. ☐ Ceilings		
7. ☐ Lights		
8. ☐ Timers		
9. ☐ Windows		
10. ☐ Outlets		
11. ☐ Toilets		
12. ☐ Water		
13. ☐ Plumbing		
14. ☐ Insects		
15. ☐ Rodents		
16. ☐ Cleanliness		

Additional comments:

Signed _____ Dated _____

#20 / Customer Comment Sheet

HOW ARE WE DOING?

We value your opinion highly and we would appreciate it if you could please let us know how you feel about our performance. Please comment on any improvements that you believe we could make to better serve you and your pets!

1. How did you find the overall service of the pet sitter?
   ☐ excellent   ☐ very good   ☐ good   ☐ poor

2. Were you pleased with the home services?
   ☐ excellent   ☐ very good   ☐ good   ☐ poor

3. Were you pleased with the pet care provided?
   ☐ excellent   ☐ very good   ☐ good   ☐ poor

4. Do you have any comments or suggestions for future services?

Thank you for your comments.

The Management

#21 / Sample Newspaper Article/Press Release

For the past ___ months, a new concept in pet care has taken this area by storm. Emerging as the leader in its field, _____ has blossomed from a one-person operation to a full-fledged business with ___ employees. The concept for petsitting is simple yet unique. When you leave home for vacation, business, etc., leave your pets in their own environment: Home Sweet Home! _____ will make daily and nightly visits to your home and provide the personal care and attention that your pampered pets are used to. The added advantage is that your plants, mail, newspapers, garbage, and lighting will all be attended to.

_____ has recently enjoyed an expansion into _____. The company president/owner, _____, believes that the key to success is being licensed, bonded and insured, being a member of the Better Business Bureau, and being able to furnish ample references, including some from area veterinarians.

If you've given up weekend trips or fretted about asking neighbors or relatives to care for your pets, then _____ is the solution to your problems. For more information and a no-charge, no-obligation consultation, call in _____ County: (_____) - _____ - _____. Thank you.

#21 / Sample Newspaper Article/Press Release

Mr. and Mrs. Johnson have just been given a wonderful opportunity to take a two-week vacation. However, the Johnsons haven't had a vacation in ten years. Why? They have two beloved pets, Samson, a five-year-old German Shepherd, and Delilah, a nine-year-old tabby cat. They could not bear to put either one of them in a kennel for one night, let alone for two weeks. What do they do?

Well, there hasn't been a ready-made solution until an enterprising entrepreneur named _____ started a new business called _____ on _____, _____ 19_____. Now all the Johnsons have to do is call _____ at _____-_____, and set up a free consultation at their home.

_____ and staff meet Samson and Delilah, and fill out a detailed file containing such information as their feeding times and specifics, a medical emergency release form, and emergency phone numbers. The Johnsons get a long list of references to call as well as being assured that _____ is fully licensed, bonded and insured.

Reassured, the Johnsons leave their precious pets and palace to _____, and go on a blissful vacation. They call every other day to see how Samson and Delilah are, and they enjoy a worry-free time. While they are gone, _____ provides lots of love and quality care for their pets, and cares meticulously for their home as well. Newspapers and mail are collected, garbage put out, and lights alternated, all giving the home a lived-in appearance. Upon their return, the Johnsons find Samson and Delilah healthy, happy and in good shape, and their home in tip-top condition.

_____ has earned a good reputation its first year with some area veterinarians on their reference list as well as host of satisfied customers and happy pets.

#22 / Sample Press Release

March 10, 1987

Palm Beach Post
2325 South Federal Highway
Delray Beach, FL 33445

Dear Sir/Madam:

I have a four-year-old UNIQUE service business that I think might be of interest to you and your readers.

I have enclosed some photographs and newspaper articles as well as my brochure and references to help familiarize you with our concept.

Although we are based in _____, we have recently expanded as far south as _____ and as far north as _____.

I'm sure you'll feel as I do that our concept is both newsworthy and noteworthy. Please contact me for further information!

Sincerely,

_____

#23 / Sample Thank You Letter To Publications

Date

Wendy Eastman, Advertising Manager
SUN NEWSPAPERS GROUP
2930 Okeechobee Blvd., Suite 207
West Palm Beach, FL 33409

Dear Wendy:

It was a pleasure meeting you yesterday! We feel confident that by advertising in your newspapers, we will see some immediate results. Thank you for all the helpful hints. As you know, starting out with an unusual concept can be difficult but with help from an experienced professional such as yourself I know I will succeed.

I look forward to working with you.

Sincerely,

_____

#24 / Sample Business Announcement to Veterinarians

Date

Veterinarian's Name
Address

Dear Dr. _____:

_____ is proud to announce its expansion
into _____. We extend to you and your customers an
open invitation to discover more about THE kennel alternative you have all been
waiting for!

_____ has been serving customers
in _____ and we have gained a tremendous reputa-
tion by providing excellent service as well as lots of tender loving care. Our service is much needed and much appreciated by our existing customers and we
hope that you will feel the same way. The good word has spread and so have
we!

_____ is fully licensed, bonded and insured, and we boast
of a long list of references including area veterinarians. What we offer is a complete pet and home care service, and above all, QUALITY attention for pets and
homeowners alike.

Please call us at ____-_____ for more information, brochures or cards, or to
meet with us personally.

Sincerely,

_____

#25 / Holiday Reminder Notices

Hi! Just a quick note to remind you that the holidays are on their way, bringing with them our busiest time of year! Please call us as soon as you have made your plans so we can reserve a place for you, our most "preferred customer." We hope that everyone is doing well and we look forward to hearing from you soon!

Thank you.

Hi! Just a short note to remind you that the _____ holidays are just around the corner. We urge you to call and make your reservations now to reserve your place. We fill up quickly at holiday time and we don't like to turn away our preferred customers. Please call as soon as you know your dates. Thank you. _____-_____

Sincerely,

_____

#26 / Complimentary Anniversary Gift Certificate

Dear Faithful Customers:

_____ would like to extend an open invitation to you and your pets to join in the celebration of our ____ year anniversary in business with a complimentary gift certificate for one free visit.

Boasting of over ____ customers from _____ and a reputation beyond reproach, we hope that you take advantage of this offer and please call to set up a no-charge, no-obligation, confidential interview.

_____ gives you "peace of mind" knowing that your pet and home are in the hands of caring professionals who are licensed, bonded, and members of the Better Business Bureau. We look forward to hearing from you and please feel free to call for any additional information you may need.

Sincerely,

_____

#27 / Sample Price Increase Letter

Date
Name
Address
City/State/Zip

Dear _____:

How are you and your pets? We hope everyone's happy and healthy. First of all, we'd like to remind you that if you plan to go away for any of the upcoming holidays, please make your reservations with us now, or as soon as possible.

The second matter that we wish to address is done so with great reluctance. Due to the sharp increases in bonding and insurance rates in our highly specialized line of work, we have no alternative but to increase our rates. The cost of providing quality care for your pets as well as your home have unfortunately risen beyond our expectations.

What this means to you in terms of dollars is that your rate per visit will go from $____ to $____. We hope that this does not inconvenience you too much. Thank you for your understanding, cooperation and support. Looking forward to hearing from you soon!

Sincerely,

_____

#28 / Sample Brochure

Back Panel

Front Panel

PET SITTING SERVICES is a family owned and operated business, experienced in all phases of pet care, ranging from pet shop and pet grooming backgrounds to personal pet owning experience.

For further information and appointments, please call Pat or Alice Doyle at 278-0593 during the day and 426-5078 evenings and weekends.

WE SPECIALIZE IN T.L.C.!!!

Pet Sitting Services
P.O. Box 489
Deerfield Bch, FL 33441

Pet Sitting Services

YOUR COMPLETE PERSONAL
PET AND HOME CARE SERVICE
LICENSED • BONDED • INSURED

Inside

The Safe, Reliable Alternative to Boarding Your Pet...	**...And Leaving Your Home Unattended and Vulnerable**

DAILY • WEEKLY • MONTHLY

WHETHER it's a weekend getaway, a long-awaited vacation, or an overnight meeting - ANY EMERGENCY OR SITUATION THAT WOULD TAKE YOU AWAY FROM HOME - **PET SITTING SERVICES** offers you the freedom and peace of mind you've never had before. Our services allow your pet (or pets) to remain in their own familiar and comfortable surroundings -
HOME SWEET HOME!

PET SERVICES INCLUDE:
- Seven-day service for the physically limited or house-bound.
- Making sure he/she is properly fed.
- Accommodating any special dietary needs or feeding times.
- Providing clean, fresh water, bedding, litter box, cage, etc.
- Administering medication at regular, prescribed intervals.
- Attending to basic grooming needs.
- Providing regular exercise, daily outings, and lots of play!!
- As often as you may need us, we'll always be there...PLUS - we will give your pet the personal love, care, and attention that they are used to.

AND, for your added convenience, we can provide certain services for your home to give it that "lived in" look...giving you the same freedom and peace of mind by eliminating your worries about general up-keep and maintenance while you are away.

HOME SERVICES INCLUDE:
- Giving your home a daily check-up.
- Plant care.
- Mail collection and newspaper pick-up.
- Clean-up and garbage removal.
- Providing adequate lighting at night to help "burglar-proof" your home.
- Keeping a record of your answering machine messages and resetting the machine.
- Starting your car daily to insure proper battery maintenance.
- Plus...any personalized service you may need - upon request.

FOR YOUR CONVENIENCE AND PLEASURE, YOU CAN CALL AS OFTEN AS YOU LIKE FOR TELEPHONE MESSAGES, MAIL RECEIVED, AND OF COURSE, TO SEE HOW YOUR PET IS DOING!!!

#29 / Accounts Receivable Log

For petsitting through _____, 19___

Customer Name	Customer #	Invoice #	$ Amount Due
1.			
2.			
3.			
4.			
5.			
6.			
7.			
8.			
9.			
10.			
11.			
12.			
13.			
14.			
15.			
16.			
17.			
18.			

Total Amount Receivable $

Revised total $
Date

Revised total $
Date

Revised total $
Date

Revised total $
Date

Prepared by   Date

#30 / Sample Invoice

INVOICE

Mail payments to: _____   All inquiries: _____

Address _____   Phone _____

_____

To: _____   Invoice # _____

Customer # _____   Date _____

Visits @ $ _____   Per visit $ _____

Previous balance $ _____

Deposit received $ _____

Balance Due $ _____

Documentation of dates and times as follows:

Dates and visits extending one week or more.

_____ Visits per day commencing _____ AM/PM and ending _____ AM/PM.

Total visits _____

Date	Times
1.	
2.	
3.	
4.	
5.	
6.	
7.	
8.	
9.	
10.	

#31 / Mileage Log Sheet

Employee/contractor

Odometer reading for week beginning

Date	Odometer Start	Odometer End	Total Miles

Total weekly mileage

Employee/contractor   Date

#32 / Weekly Motor Vehicle Expense Report

Week Ending

Date	Gas $	Oil $	Tolls $	Misc. $

Totals: Gas $ Oil $ Tolls $ Misc $

All receipts must accompany reports.

Total weekly expenses $

Signed   Dated

#33 / Request for Payment Letter

Date

To
Address
City/St/Zip

Re: Invoice # _____ Outstanding Amount $_____

Dear _____:

How are you and the group? All doing well I hope. While reviewing my records, I find that I show no record of payment for the invoice dated _____ through _____ in the amount of $_____. This may be an oversight. Could you please let me know the check number and date paid.? I have been wondering also if perhaps it had been mailed to the wrong address. Thank you and please call again soon when you plan your next trip.

Sincerely,

_____

#34 / Late Payment Reminder

Date

To
Address
City/State/Zip

You have always been a valued account with an excellent record of prompt payment and we want you to know that we appreciate that. Your account, however, is now past due in the amount of $_____. We are reminding you of this knowing you would not generally permit your account to remain in arrears and will want to correct this oversight. We look forward to receipt of your check.

Very truly yours,

_____

#35 / Notice of Dishonored Check

_____
Date
_____
To   Customer #
_____
Name
_____
Address
_____
City/State   Zip
_____

Payment on your check no. ____ in the amount of $____ tendered to us on _____ 19__ has been refused by your bank. We have verified with your bank that there are still insufficient funds to pay the check.

We request that you replace this check with cash or a certified check payment. A $____ nsf charge must also be included, making the total due $_____.

Please pay upon receipt of this letter. Thank you.

Very truly yours,

_____

#36 / Employment Inquiry Response Letter

Thank you for inquiring about a position with _____. We have had a tremendous response to the concept of our pet and home care service and we look forward to expanding and hopefully bringing you into one of the most fulfilling, not to mention fun and exciting fields of animal care today. Please find the enclosed application and brochure on the company to help you get a better idea of the many services that we offer to our customers and to familiarize you with what we really do.

Our number one priority is the care and comfort of the pets that we are entrusted to care for. If you have any additional questions, please call and we will be more than happy to answer them. Thanks again for your interest and we expect to hear from you soon.

Sincerely,

_____

#37 / Application for Employment

1. Name
_____

2. Address
_____

3. City/St/Zip
_____

4. How many years have you lived at the aforementioned address?
   Years _____ Months _____ Do you ☐ Rent? ☐ Own?

Landlord's name and phone number
_____

5. Do you have a valid drivers license? ☐ Yes ☐ No

Drivers license number _____ Renewal year _____

6. Car make and model _____ Year _____ Auto tag# _____

7. Please list your nearest relative, address, phone number:

_____

8. Car insurance company:

   Policy # _____

9. You will be required to obtain an identification card from the division of motor vehicles or local police department. Is this agreeable to you? ☐ Yes ☐ No

10. Additional references are required. Please list three people that you have known five years or more. No relatives. Please list their name, address, phone number and relationship.

1. _____

2. _____

3. _____

I certify that all of the above facts are true and verifiable and hereby give permission to check all of the above statements and references.

_____

Signed _____ Date _____

#38 / Addendum to Employment Application

1. Name _____

   Address _____

   City _____ State _____ Zip _____

2. How many years _____ months _____ have you lived at the aforementioned address stated on your application?

3. Do you ☐ Own ☐ Rent your present home or apartment?

4. List your two previous addresses:

   #1 Address _____

   City _____ State _____ Zip _____

   #2 Address _____

   City _____ State _____ Zip _____

5. Car make _____ Model _____

   Year _____ Auto tag number _____

6. Do you possess a valid driver's license? ☐ Yes ☐ No

7. Driver's license number _____

8. Additional references are required. Please list three people whom you have known at least five years, their relationship to you, their address, place of business and telephone numbers. No relatives.

   1. _____

   2. _____

   3. _____

9. In case of emergency, list your nearest relative, address, telephone number:

10. This position requires driving to and from your designated job. Therefore, it is necessary that you have in existence ample car insurance while you are working for _____. Please state your insurance company and policy number for our records:

Type of coverage on your car? _____

11. If hired or contracted by _____ you will be required to obtain a police identification card from the state drivers license bureau. Is this agreeable to you? ☐ Yes ☐ No

#38, continued

12. Have you ever been arrested? ☐ Yes ☐ No Convicted of a crime? ☐ Yes ☐ No
13. Have you ever been fired? ☐ Yes ☐ No   If so, Why?

_____

14. Are you bondable? ☐ Yes ☐ No

15. Has your driver's license ever been revoked? ☐ Yes ☐ No

16. List the names and addresses of the schools you have attended and the time periods:

High School
_____
Address   Years attended
_____
Did you graduate? ☐ Yes ☐ No

College or Vocational School
_____
Address
_____
Years attended
_____
Did you graduate? ☐ Yes ☐ No

I certify that the above facts are true and verifiable. I hereby give _____
permission to verify all information and statements. I understand that if any statements
above are found to be untrue or if I have ommitted any pertinent information, my services
will be terminated immediately.

_____
Signed   Date

#39 / Consent To Release of Employment Information

The undersigned _____ (employee/contractor) hereby authorizes the release of the employment information checked below:

_____

☐ Salary: _____

☐ Position: _____

☐ Department: _____

☐ Supervisor's name: _____

☐ Dates of employment: _____

☐ Name under which you worked: _____

☐ Garnishes if any: _____

☐ Reasons for leaving: _____

☐ Medical/accidents/illness reports: _____

☐ Other:

_____   _____
Employee/contractor signature   Date

_____   _____
Employer/owner   Date

#40 / Employment Contract

1. This Agreement made this _____ day of _____ 19___, between _____, having its principal place of business at _____, hereinafter referred to as the Employer, and _____ of _____, hereinafter referred to as Employee, beginning on the _____ day of _____ 19___, however, this Agreement may be terminated earlier as hereinafter provided.

Duties of the Employee

2. The duties to be performed by the Employee shall be determined from time to time by the President or the Board of Directors of the Employer and promptly communicated to the Employee.

3. In addition to the foregoing duties, the Employee shall perform such other work as may be assigned to him/her subject to the instructions, directions and control of the Employer, provided only such additional duties shall be during the hours designated and specified in this contract.

4. The Employee shall devote his or her productive time, ability, and attention to the business of the Employer during the term of this contract. The Employee shall not directly or indirectly render any services of a business, commercial or professional nature to any other person or organization, whether for compensation or otherwise, without written consent of the Employer.

5. As compensation for services rendered under this contract, the Employee shall be entitled to payment from the Employer at the rate of $_____ per hour to be paid weekly on the _____ day of the week.

6. The Employer, in accordance with rules and regulations that may be issued from time to time, shall reimburse the Employee for travel expenses at $_____ cents per mile.

7. The Employee, during the term of employment under this Agreement, will have access to and become familiar with various trade secrets. The Employee shall not disclose any of the aforesaid trade secrets, directly or indirectly, or use them in any way, either during the term of this agreement or any time thereafter, except if required in the course of his or her employment.

8. During the term of this contract, the Employee shall not directly or indirectly, either as Employee, consultant, agent, principal or in any representative or individual capacity, engage or participate in any business that is in competition in any manner whatsoever with the business of the Employer.

#40, continued

9. On consideration of the Employer employing the Employee in a position, wherein he or she will gain specialized knowledge and experience and will establish personal relationships with Employer's customers, the Employee will agree to as follows:

On termination of the employment, whether by termination of this Agreement, by discharge, or otherwise, the Employee shall not enter into or engage generally in direct competition with the Employer in the business of the Employer, directly or indirectly, within the existing market area of the Employer in the counties of _____, _____, _____, in the State of _____ or in any future marketing area of the Employer in the business of the Employer, for a period of ____ years after the date of termination of this Contract. This covenant on the part of the Employee shall be construed as an Agreement independent of any other provision of this Agreement; and the existence of any claim or cause of action of the Employee against the Employer, whether predicted on this Contract or otherwise, shall not constitute a defense to the enforcement by the Employer of this covenant. In the event of a breach by the Employee of his/her obligations under this restrictive covenant, the Employee acknowledges that the Employer will not have an adequate remedy at law and shall be entitled to such equitable and injunctive relief which may be available to restrain the Employee from violation of the provisions hereof. Nothing herein shall be construed as prohibiting the Employer from pursuing any other remedies available for such breach or threatened breach, including recovery of damages from the Employee.

10. The Employee agrees that he/she will furnish all information and take any other steps necessary to enable the Employer to obtain a fidelity bond conditioned on the rendering of a true account by the Employee of all monies, goods, or other property which may come into the custody, charge, or possession of the Employee during the term of this employment. All premiums on the Bond are to be paid by the Employer. Failure by the Employee to qualify for such bond within 10 days from the date of this Agreement will result in an immediate termination of this employment contract.

11. The Employment of the Employee shall continue only as long as the services rendered are satisfactory to the Employer, regardless of any other provision contained in this Agreement. The Employer shall be the sole judge as to whether the services of the Employee are satisfactory.

12. If the Employee willfully breaches or habitually neglects the duties which he/she is required to perform under the terms of this Agreement, the Employer may at his option, terminate the Agreement by giving written notice of termination to the Employee without prejudice to any other remedy to which Employer may be entitled either at law, in equity, or under this Agreement.

#40, continued

13. This Agreement may be terminated by either party giving 10 days written notice to the other party.

14. In the event of breach of this Agreement by either the Employer or the Employee resulting in damages to the other party, that party may recover from the party breaching the Agreement any and all damages that may be sustained.

15. Any notices to be given hereunder by either party may be elected either by personal delivery in writing or by mail, registered or certified, postage prepaid with return receipt requested. Mailed notices shall be addressed to the parties at the addresses appearing in the introductory paragraph of this agreement, but each party may change his or her address by written notice in accordance with this Paragraph.

16. This Agreement supersedes any and all agreements, either oral or in writing, between the parties hereto with respect to the employment of the Employee by the Employer and contains all of the covenants and agreements between parties with respect to such employment in any manner whatsoever.

17. This Agreement shall be governed by and construed with the laws of the State of
_____

18. If any action at law or in equity is necessary to enforce or interpret the terms of this agreement, the prevailing party shall be entitled to reasonable attorneys fees, costs, and necessary disbursements in addition to any other relief to which he may be entitled.

19. It is expressly agreed that the Employee shall have no right or authority at any time to make any contract or binding promise of any nature on behalf of the Employer, without the express consent of the Employer.

Signed at the City of _____, State of _____, on the day and year first above written with intent to be legally bound.

EMPLOYER:

By: _____

EMPLOYEE:

By: _____

#41 / Independent Contractor Acknowledgment

The undersigned hereby enters into an independent contractor arrangement or affiliation with _____ Company, as of this date.

In accordance therewith the undersigned confirms:

1. The undersigned is an independent contractor and is not an employee, agent, partner or joint venturer of or with the Company.

2. The undersigned shall not be entitled to participate in any vacation, medical, or other fringe benefits of the Company and shall not make claim of entitlement to any such program or benefit.

3. The undersigned shall be solely responsible for the payment of withholding taxes, Social Security taxes and other such tax deductions on any earnings or payments made. The Company shall withhold no such payroll tax deductions from any payments due. The undersigned agrees to indemnify and reimburse the Company from any claim or assessment by any taxing authority arising from this paragraph.

Signed _____ Dated _____
                 Contractor

Signed _____ Dated _____
              Owner/President

#42 / Employee Non-Compete Agreement

The undersigned employee hereby agrees not to directly or indirectly compete with the business of the company during the period of employment or independent contractor status and for a period of _____ years following termination of employment and notwithstanding the cause and reason for termination.

The term **"not to compete"** as used herein shall mean that the employee or independent contractor shall not own, manage, operate, consult to or be employed in a business substantially similar to or competitive with the present business of the company or such other business activity in which the company may engage during the term of employment.

The employee acknowledges that the company shall or may in reliance of this agreement provide access to trade secrets, customers and other confidential data and that the provisions of this agreement are reasonably necessary to protect the company and its good will.

This agreement shall be binding upon and ensure to the benefit of the parties, their successors, assigns and personal representatives.

Signed _____ Dated _____

                Employee/Contractor

Company name

Signed _____ Dated _____

                Owner/President

#43 / Confidentiality Agreement

Agreement and acknowledgement between _____ (the Company) and _____ (the Undersigned) whereas, the Company agrees to furnish the Undersigned access to confidential information relating to the affairs of the Company for purposes of gaining entry to the homes that the Company is entrusted to care for and, whereas, the Undersigned agrees to review, examine, inspect, or obtain such information only for purposes described above, and to otherwise hold such information confidential and secret pursuant to the terms of this agreement.

Be it known, that the Company has or shall furnish to the Undersigned certain confidential information.

1. The Undersigned agrees to hold all confidential and proprietary information or trade secrets in trust and confidence and agrees that it shall be used for the contemplated purpose, and shall not be used for any other purpose or disclosed to a third party.

2. No copies will be made or information retained of any information supplied.

3. At the conclusions of our discussions, or upon demand by the Company, all information, including written notes, photographs, or memoranda shall be returned to the Company.

4. This information shall not be disclosed to any employee, consultant or third party.

5. It is understood that the undersigned shall have no obligation with respect to any information known or generally known within the industry prior to the date of this agreement, or that shall become common knowledge within the industry thereafter.

6. The Undersigned acknowledges the information disclosed herein is proprietary or trade secrets and in the event of any breach, the Company shall be entitled to injunctive relief as cumulative and not necessarily successive remedy.

7. This agreement shall be binding upon and inure to the benefit of the parties, their successors and assigns.

Signed _____ Dated _____
         Employee/Contractor

Signed _____ Dated _____
         Owner/President

#44 / Independent Contractor Agreement

This agreement entered into this _____ day of _____ 19____, between _____ and_____, doing business as a petsitting service, under the name of _____, hereafter called _____, and _____, hereafter called contractor, witnesseth whereas _____ are engaged in the business of _____ whereas, _____ have a large number of customers who require their services, whereas, contractor is desirous of entering into an independent contractor status with _____ whereby he or she will engage in the business of petsitting for customers of _____.

Now, therefore, for and in consideration of the mutual promises hereinafter expressed, the receipt and sufficiency whereof are hereby acknowledged, the parties agree as follows:

1. Obligations of _____

a) _____ will instruct contractor for an appropriate period of time in the proper way to perform these services.

b) At the beginning of each week, _____ will provide contractor with a schedule of jobs to perform for customers of _____ along with the instructions from these customers as to the manner of pet sitting that needs to be performed.

c) At the end of each week, _____ will pay to the contractor compensation for the work performed during that week at the rate of $ _____ per hour.

d) Other than the appropriate instruction and providing contractor with a schedule of jobs at the beginning of each week, _____ will not be responsible for any other assistance to the contractor in the performance of his or her petsitting work for their customers.

2. Obligations of Contractor

a) Contractor will perform all petsitting services required during each week for customers of _____ and will do so pursuant to the instructions of each such customer, per the customer file.

b) Contractor will record the number of hours he or she works for each customer of _____ during the week and submit to _____ a bill for payment of services based on the total hours worked multiplied by $ _____ per hour.

#44, continued

3. Independent Contractor

a) This agreement does not make contractor an agent, legal representative, joint venturer, or partner of _____

b) Contractor understands and agrees that he or she is an independent contractor and cannot authorize any contracts or agreements on behalf of _____ or to create any obligation expressed or implied on behalf of _____

c) It is expressly agreed that contractor is not an employee of _____

d) Contractor agrees that he or she will, at his or her expense, make all payments and prepare all returns required by the Social Security Act and the Income Tax Act, whether federal or state. _____ Assumes no responsibility for making any such reports or payments to the Social Security Administration or to federal or state governments for income tax.

e) As an independent contractor, contractor acknowledges that he or she is not covered by worker's compensation of the state of _____

Signed in the city of _____, state of _____, on the ____ day of _____, 199___, written with intent to be legally bound.

Signed _____ Dated _____
                Contractor

Signed _____ Dated _____
             Owner/President

#45 / Independent Contractor Pay Sheet

Contractor name _____

Contractor Social Security number _____

Pay period week ending _____

Recorded hours _____

Recorded mileage _____

Total hours _____

Hourly rate _____

Per job rate _____

Total amount earned $ _____

Amount paid $ _____

Date paid _____

Check # _____

Signed _____ Dated _____
　　　　　　Independent Contractor

Signed _____ Dated _____
　　　　　　Owner/President

#46 / Night Shift Agreement

Employee/contractor name _____

A night shift is or may be required to meet present or future work schedules. All new employees or contractors are hired with the understanding that they are willing and able to work nights.

Please answer the following questions:

1. Do you have any physical disability or impairment that would interfere with your working at night? ☐ Yes   ☐ No

2. Are there any home conditions that would interfere with your working at night? ☐ Yes   ☐ No

I acknowledge that the offer of employment with _____
made to me upon this date was conditional upon my acceptance of night assignments if required.

Signed _____ Dated _____
                    Petsitter

Signed _____ Dated _____
                Owner/President

#47 / Employee/Contractor Weekly Time Sheet and Mileage Report

Employee/Contractor Name _____

Client	Odometer Start/Odometer End	Time In/Out	Total Mi./Hrs.

Total miles   Total hours

Total $ miles   Total $ hours

#48/ Resignation

Date _____

To _____

Please be advised that the undersigned hereby tenders resignation as petsitter for _____, effective herewith. All supplies, customer files and applicable information has been surrendered to the employer upon submission of this resignation.

Signed _____ Dated _____
　　　　　Petsitter

This foregoing resignation is hereby accepted this _____ day of _____ 19___.

Signed _____ Dated _____
　　　　Owner/President

Appendix Two

Additional Information

The following is a listing of holidays that are often celebrated. You may be in demand during these times and should be aware of when they fall.

JANUARY
New Year's Day
Martin Luther King Jr.'s Birthday

FEBRUARY
Valentine's Day
President's Day
Washington's Birthday

MARCH
St. Patrick's Day

APRIL
Good Friday
Passover
Palm Sunday

MAY
Mother's Day
Memorial Day
Armed Forces Day

JUNE
Father's Day
Flag Day
Children's Day
Summer Vacations Begin

JULY
Independence Day
Summer Vacations

AUGUST
Summer Vacations

SEPTEMBER
Labor Day

OCTOBER
Yom Kippur
Columbus Day
Halloween

NOVEMBER
Veteran's Day
Thanksgiving

DECEMBER
Pearl Harbor Day
Christmas
New Year's Eve
Winter Begins

* Please obtain a calendar for the exact dates of the above holidays.

IRS Information Telephone Numbers

The following are telephone numbers in each of the states for IRS information. We have tried to provide the most current information in the printing of this book, however, some numbers may have changed after press time.

ALABAMA
1-800-829-1040

ALASKA
Anchorage 907-561-7484
Elsewhere 1-800-829-1040

ARIZONA
Phoenix 602-257-1233
Elsewhere 1-800-829-1040

ARKANSAS
1-800-929-1040

CALIFORNIA
Oakland 415-839-1040
San Francisco 415-839-1040
Elsewhere 1-800-829-1040

COLORADO
Denver 303-825-7041
Elsewhere 1-800-829-1040

CONNECTICUT
1-800-829-1040

DELAWARE
1-800-829-1040

DISTRICT OF COLUMBIA
1-800-829-1040

FLORIDA
Jacksonville 904-354-1760
Elsewhere 1-800-829-1040

GEORGIA
Atlanta 404-522-0050
Elsewhere 1-800-829-1040

HAWAII
Oahu 808-541-1040
Elsewhere 1-800-829-1040

IDAHO
1-800-820-1040

ILLINOIS
Chicago 708-435-1040
1-312-435-1040
Elsewhere 1-800-829-1040

INDIANA
Indianapolis 317-226-5477
Elsewhere 1-800-829-1040

IOWA
Des Moines 515-283-0523
Elsewhere 1-800-829-1040

KANSAS
1-800-829-1040

KENTUCKY
1-800-829-1040

LOUISIANA
1-800-829-1040

MAINE
1-800-829-1040

MARYLAND
Baltimore 301-962-2590
Elsewhere 1-800-829-1040

MASSACHUSETTS
Boston 617-523-1040
Elsewhere 1-800-829-1040

MICHIGAN
Detroit 313-237-0800
Elsewhere 1-800-829-1040

MINNESOTA
Minneapolis 612-644-7515
St. Paul 644-7515
Elsewhere 1-800-829-1040

MISSISSIPPI
1-800-829-1040

MISSOURI
St. Louis 314-342-1040
Elsewhere 1-800-820-1040

MONTANA
1-800-829-1040

NEBRASKA
Omaha 402-422-1500
Elsewhere 1-800-829-1040

NEVADA
1-800-829-1040

NEW HAMPSHIRE
1-800-820-1040

NEW JERSEY
1-800-829-1040

NEW MEXICO
1-800-820-1040

NEW YORK
Bronx 212-732-0100
Brooklyn 718-596-3770
Buffalo 716-685-5432
Manhattan 212-732-0100
Queens 718-596-3770
Staten Island 718-596-3770
Elsewhere 1-800-829-1040

NORTH CAROLINA
1-800-829-1040

NORTH DAKOTA
1-800-829-1040

OHIO
Cincinnati 513-621-6281
Cleveland 216-522-3000
Elsewhere 1-800-820-1040

OKLAHOMA
1-800-829-1040

OREGON
Portland 503-221-3960
Elsewhere 1-800-829-1040

PENNSYLVANIA
Philadelphia 215-574-9900
Pittsburgh 412-281-0112
Elsewhere 1-800-829-1040

PUERTO RICO
San Juan Metro Area
809-766-5040
Isla 809-768-5549

RHODE ISLAND
1-800-829-1040

SOUTH CAROLINA
1-800-829-1040

SOUTH DAKOTA
1-800-829-1040

TENNESSEE
Nashville 615-259-4601
Elsewhere 1-800 829-1040

TEXAS
Dallas 214-742-2440
Houston 713-541-0440
Elsewhere 1-800-829-1040

UTAH
1-800-829-1040

VERMONT
1-800-829-1040

VIRGINIA
Richmond 804-649-2361

WASHINGTON
Seattle 206-442-1040
Elsewhere 1-800-829-1040

WEST VIRGINIA
1-800-829-1040

WISCONSIN
Milwaukee 414-271-3780
Elsewhere 1-800-829-1040

WYOMING
1-800-829-1040

Phone help for the hearing impaired with TDD equipment: All areas in U.S. including Alaska, Hawaii, Virgin Islands and Puerto Rico 1-800-829-4059.

Hours of Operation
8:00 A.M. to 6:30 P.M. EST, January 1-April 4
9:00 A.M. to 7:30 P.M. EDT, April 5-April 15
9:00 A.M. to 5:30 P.M. EDT, April 16-October 24
8:00 A.M. to 4:30 P.M. EST, October 25-December 31

Index